CONTENTS

1.ARRAY OPERATIONS

1.1. Create an array

```c
#include <stdio.h>
int main()
{
    // Declare an array of integers with a fixed size
    int numbers[5];
    // Assign values to the array elements
    numbers[0] = 10;
    numbers[1] = 20;
    numbers[2] = 30;
    numbers[3] = 40;
    numbers[4] = 50;
    // Access and print the elements of the array
    printf("Elements of the array: ");
    for (int i = 0; i < 5; i++) {
        printf("%d ", numbers[i]);
    }
    return 0;
}
```

In this example:

- An array named numbers of integers is declared with a fixed size of 5 elements.
- Values are assigned to each element of the array.
- The for loop is used to access and print the elements of the array.

Output:

Elements of the array: 10 20 30 40 50

You can adjust the size of the array and the values assigned to suit your specific requirements.

1.2. Initialize elements in an array

```c
#include <stdio.h>
int main()
{
    // Declare and initialize an array of integers
    int numbers[] = {10, 20, 30, 40, 50};
    // Access and print the elements of the array
    printf("Elements of the array: ");
    for (int i = 0; i < 5; i++)
{

    printf("%d ", numbers[i]);
}
    return 0;
}
```

In this example:

- An array named numbers is declared and initialized with values {10, 20, 30, 40, 50}.
- The for loop is used to access and print the elements of the array.

Output:

Elements of the array: 10 20 30 40 50

This method of initialization is concise and useful, especially when you know the values at compile time. The size of the array is automatically determined based on the number of initialized elements.

1.3. Insert element in an array

To insert an element into an array in C programming, you typically need to shift the existing elements to make room for the new element. Here's an example of how you can insert an element at a specific position in an array:

```c
#include <stdio.h>
// Function to insert an element at a specified position in the array
void insertElement(int arr[], int *size, int position, int value)
{
    // Check if the position is valid
    if (position < 0 || position > *size)
    {
        printf("Invalid position for insertion.\n");
        return;
    }
    // Shift elements to make room for the new element
    for (int i = *size - 1; i >= position; i--)
    {
        arr[i + 1] = arr[i];
    }
    // Insert the new element at the specified position
    arr[position] = value;

    // Increase the size of the array
    (*size)++;
}
int main()
{
    int numbers[10] = {10, 20, 30, 40, 50};
    int size = 5; // Initial size of the array
    // Print the original array
```

```c
    printf("Original Array: ");
    for (int i = 0; i < size; i++)
{

        printf("%d ", numbers[i]);

    }
    printf("\n");
    // Insert a new element (e.g., 25) at position 2
    insertElement(numbers, &size, 2, 25);
    // Print the modified array
    printf("Modified Array: ");
    for (int i = 0; i < size; i++)
{

        printf("%d ", numbers[i]);

    }
    printf("\n");
    return 0;

}
```

In this example, the insertElement function is used to insert a new value at a specified position in the array. The existing elements are shifted to accommodate the new element. The program then demonstrates the insertion by printing the original and modified arrays.

1.4.Delete element in an array

To delete an element from an array in C programming, you need to shift the remaining elements to fill the gap created by the deleted element. Here's an example of how you can delete an element from a specific position in an array:

```c
#include <stdio.h>
// Function to delete an element at a specified position in the array
void deleteElement(int arr[], int *size, int position)
{
    // Check if the position is valid
    if (position < 0 || position >= *size)
    {
        printf("Invalid position for deletion.\n");
        return;
    }
    // Shift elements to fill the gap created by the deleted element
    for (int i = position; i < *size - 1; i++)
    {
        arr[i] = arr[i + 1];
    }
    // Decrease the size of the array
    (*size)--;
}
int main()
{
    int numbers[10] = {10, 20, 30, 40, 50};
    int size = 5; // Initial size of the array
    // Print the original array
    printf("Original Array: ");
    for (int i = 0; i < size; i++)
    {
```

```c
        printf("%d ", numbers[i]);
    }
    printf("\n");
    // Delete the element at position 2
    deleteElement(numbers, &size, 2);
    // Print the modified array
    printf("Modified Array: ");
    for (int i = 0; i < size; i++)
{
        printf("%d ", numbers[i]);
    }
    printf("\n");
    return 0;
}
```

In this example, the deleteElement function is used to delete an element from a specified position in the array. The remaining elements are shifted to fill the gap left by the deleted element. The program then demonstrates the deletion by printing the original and modified arrays.

1.5. Search element in an array

To search for an element in an array in C programming, you can use a loop to iterate through the array and check if the desired element is present. Here's an example:

```c
#include <stdio.h>
// Function to search for an element in the array
int searchElement(const int arr[], int size, int key)
{
  for (int i = 0; i < size; i++)
{
    if (arr[i] == key)
{
      return i; // Return the index if the element is found
    }
  }
  return -1; // Return -1 if the element is not found
}
int main()
{
  int numbers[] = {10, 20, 30, 40, 50};
  int size = 5; // Size of the array
  int key;
  // Print the original array
  printf("Original Array: ");
  for (int i = 0; i < size; i++)
{
    printf("%d ", numbers[i]);
  }
  printf("\n");
  // Input the element to search
  printf("Enter the element to search: ");
```

```c
    scanf("%d", &key);
    // Search for the element
    int index = searchElement(numbers, size, key);
    // Check and display the result
    if (index != -1)
{
        printf("Element %d found at index %d.\n", key, index);
    }
else
{
        printf("Element %d not found in the array.\n", key);
}
    return 0;
}
```

In this example:

- The searchElement function takes an array, its size, and the element to search for as parameters.
- It iterates through the array using a loop and returns the index of the element if found, or -1 if not found.
- The main function demonstrates the usage by searching for a user-input element in the array and displaying the result.

This is a basic linear search algorithm. If the array is sorted, more efficient search algorithms like binary search can be used.

1.6. Sum elements in an array

To find the sum of elements in an array in C programming, you can use a loop to iterate through the array and accumulate the values. Here's an example:

```c
#include <stdio.h>
// Function to calculate the sum of elements in the array
int sumArray(const int arr[], int size)
{
   int sum = 0;
   for (int i = 0; i < size; i++)
{
     sum += arr[i];
   }
   return sum;
}
int main()
{
   int numbers[] = {10, 20, 30, 40, 50};
   int size = 5; // Size of the array
   // Print the original array
   printf("Array: ");
   for (int i = 0; i < size; i++)
{
     printf("%d ", numbers[i]);
   }
   printf("\n");
   // Calculate the sum of elements in the array
   int arraySum = sumArray(numbers, size);
   // Display the result
   printf("Sum of elements: %d\n", arraySum);
   return 0;
```

}

In this example:

- The sumArray function takes an array and its size as parameters.
- It iterates through the array using a loop and accumulates the values in the sum variable.
- The main function demonstrates the usage by calculating and displaying the sum of elements in the array.

1.7.Average elements in an array

To find the average of elements in an array in C programming, you can first calculate the sum of the elements using a loop, and then divide the sum by the number of elements. Here's an example:

```c
#include <stdio.h>
// Function to calculate the average of elements in the array
double averageArray(const int arr[], int size)
{
    int sum = 0;
    // Calculate the sum of elements
    for (int i = 0; i < size; i++)
    {
        sum += arr[i];
    }
    // Calculate and return the average
    return (double)sum / size;
}
int main()
{
    int numbers[] = {10, 20, 30, 40, 50};
    int size = 5; // Size of the array
    // Print the original array
    printf("Array: ");
    for (int i = 0; i < size; i++)
    {
        printf("%d ", numbers[i]);
    }
    printf("\n");
    // Calculate the average of elements in the array
    double arrayAverage = averageArray(numbers, size);
```

```c
// Display the result
printf("Average of elements: %.2f\n", arrayAverage);
return 0;
}
```

In this example:

- The averageArray function takes an array and its size as parameters.
- It calculates the sum of elements using a loop.
- The average is calculated by dividing the sum by the number of elements (size).
- The main function demonstrates the usage by calculating and displaying the average of elements in the array.

Note that the result is stored as a double to account for the possibility of fractional values in the average. Adjust the format specifier in the printf statement accordingly if you want a different precision in the output.

1.8. Find the maximum element in an array

To find the maximum element in an array in C programming, you can iterate through the array, keeping track of the maximum element found so far. Here's an example:

```c
#include <stdio.h>
// Function to find the maximum element in the array
int findMax(const int arr[], int size)
{
    // Check if the array is empty
    if (size == 0) {
        printf("Array is empty.\n");
        return -1; // Return a special value to indicate an empty array
    }
    int max = arr[0]; // Assume the first element is the maximum
    // Iterate through the array to find the maximum element
    for (int i = 1; i < size; i++)
    {
        if (arr[i] > max)
        {
            max = arr[i];
        }
    }
    return max;
}
int main()
{
    int numbers[] = {10, 20, 30, 40, 50};
    int size = 5; // Size of the array
    // Print the original array
    printf("Array: ");
    for (int i = 0; i < size; i++)
```

```c
{
    printf("%d ", numbers[i]);
}
printf("\n");
// Find the maximum element in the array
int maxElement = findMax(numbers, size);
// Display the result
if (maxElement != -1)
{
    printf("Maximum element: %d\n", maxElement);
}
return 0;
}
```

In this example:

- The findMax function takes an array and its size as parameters.
- It initializes the max variable with the first element of the array and iterates through the array to find the maximum element.
- The main function demonstrates the usage by finding and displaying the maximum element in the array.

The special value -1 is returned if the array is empty, and you can adjust this behavior based on your specific requirements.

1.9. Find the minimum element in an array

To find the minimum element in an array in C programming, you can iterate through the array, keeping track of the minimum element found so far. Here's an example:

```c
#include <stdio.h>
// Function to find the minimum element in the array
int findMin(const int arr[], int size)
{
  // Check if the array is empty
  if (size == 0)
  {
    printf("Array is empty.\n");
    return -1; // Return a special value to indicate an empty array
  }
  int min = arr[0]; // Assume the first element is the minimum
  // Iterate through the array to find the minimum element
  for (int i = 1; i < size; i++)
  {
    if (arr[i] < min)
      {
      min = arr[i];
      }
  }
  return min;
}
int main()
{
  int numbers[] = {30, 10, 50, 20, 40};
  int size = 5; // Size of the array
  // Print the original array
  printf("Array: ");
```

```c
    for (int i = 0; i < size; i++)
    {
        printf("%d ", numbers[i]);
    }
    printf("\n");
    // Find the minimum element in the array
    int minElement = findMin(numbers, size);
    // Display the result
    if (minElement != -1)
    {
        printf("Minimum element: %d\n", minElement);
    }
    return 0;
}
```

In this example:

- The findMin function takes an array and its size as parameters.
- It initializes the min variable with the first element of the array and iterates through the array to find the minimum element.
- The main function demonstrates the usage by finding and displaying the minimum element in the array.

The special value -1 is returned if the array is empty, and you can adjust this behavior based on your specific requirements.

1.10. Merge two sorted Arrays

To merge two sorted arrays in C programming, you can use a simple algorithm that compares elements from both arrays and puts the smaller element into a new array. Here's an example:

```c
#include <stdio.h>
// Function to merge two sorted arrays
void mergeArrays(const int arr1[], int size1, const int arr2[], int size2, int result[])
{
    int i = 0, j = 0, k = 0;
    // Compare elements from both arrays and merge
    while (i < size1 && j < size2)
    {
        if (arr1[i] < arr2[j])
        {
            result[k++] = arr1[i++];
        } else {
            result[k++] = arr2[j++];
        }
    }
    // Copy the remaining elements of arr1, if any
    while (i < size1)
    {
        result[k++] = arr1[i++];
    }
    // Copy the remaining elements of arr2, if any
    while (j < size2)
    {
        result[k++] = arr2[j++];
    }
}
```

```c
int main()
{
    int arr1[] = {1, 3, 5, 7, 9};
    int size1 = sizeof(arr1) / sizeof(arr1[0]);
    int arr2[] = {2, 4, 6, 8, 10};
    int size2 = sizeof(arr2) / sizeof(arr2[0]);
    int mergedArray[size1 + size2];
    // Merge the two sorted arrays
    mergeArrays(arr1, size1, arr2, size2, mergedArray);
    // Display the merged array
    printf("Merged Array: ");
    for (int i = 0; i < size1 + size2; i++)
    {

        printf("%d ", mergedArray[i]);
    }
    printf("\n");
    return 0;
}
```

In this example:

- The mergeArrays function takes two sorted arrays (arr1 and arr2), their sizes, and an array to store the merged result.
- The while loop compares elements from both arrays and puts the smaller one into the result array.
- The remaining elements from both arrays are copied into the result array.
- The main function demonstrates the usage by merging two sorted arrays and displaying the merged result.

This algorithm has a time complexity of O(size1 + size2), where size1 and size2 are the sizes of the input arrays.

2.SEARCHING TECHNIQUES

2.1.Binary search

Binary search is an efficient algorithm to search for an element in a sorted array. Here's an example of implementing binary search in C:

```c
#include <stdio.h>
// Function to perform binary search on a sorted array
int binarySearch(const int arr[], int size, int key)
{
   int left = 0;
   int right = size - 1;
   while (left <= right)
{

      int mid = left + (right - left) / 2;
      // Check if the key is present at the middle
      if (arr[mid] == key)

         {
         return mid; // Key found, return its index
      }
      // If the key is smaller, ignore the right half
      else if (arr[mid] > key)
{

         right = mid - 1;
      }
      // If the key is larger, ignore the left half
      else
{

         left = mid + 1;
      }
   }
```

```c
    return -1; // Key not found
}
int main()
{
    int numbers[] = {10, 20, 30, 40, 50, 60, 70};
    int size = sizeof(numbers) / sizeof(numbers[0]);
    int key;
    // Print the sorted array
    printf("Sorted Array: ");
    for (int i = 0; i < size; i++)
    {
        printf("%d ", numbers[i]);
    }
    printf("\n");
    // Input the element to search
    printf("Enter the element to search: ");
    scanf("%d", &key);
    // Perform binary search
    int index = binarySearch(numbers, size, key);
    // Check and display the result
    if (index != -1)
    {
        printf("Element %d found at index %d.\n", key, index);
    } else
    {
        printf("Element %d not found in the array.\n", key);
    }
    return 0;
}
```

In this example:

- The binarySearch function takes a sorted array, its size, and the key to search for.
- It initializes two pointers, left and right, to define the search space.
- The while loop continues until the search space is valid.
- If the key is equal to the middle element, it is found, and the index is returned.
- If the key is smaller, the search is continued in the left half; otherwise, in the right half.
- The main function demonstrates the usage by searching for a user-input element in the sorted array and displaying the result.

Binary search has a time complexity of O(log n), making it more efficient than linear search for large sorted arrays.

2.2.Linear search

Linear search is a simple algorithm to find an element in an array by sequentially checking each element. Here's an example of implementing linear search in C:

```c
#include <stdio.h>
// Function to perform linear search in an array
int linearSearch(const int arr[], int size, int key)
{
  for (int i = 0; i < size; i++)
{

    if (arr[i] == key)
{

        return i; // Key found, return its index

      }

    }
  return -1; // Key not found

}
int main()
{
  int numbers[] = {10, 20, 30, 40, 50, 60, 70};
  int size = sizeof(numbers) / sizeof(numbers[0]);
  int key;
  // Print the array
  printf("Array: ");
  for (int i = 0; i < size; i++)
{

    printf("%d ", numbers[i]);

  }
  printf("\n");
  // Input the element to search
  printf("Enter the element to search: ");
```

```c
    scanf("%d", &key);
    // Perform linear search
    int index = linearSearch(numbers, size, key);
    // Check and display the result
    if (index != -1)
{
        printf("Element %d found at index %d.\n", key, index);
    } else
{
        printf("Element %d not found in the array.\n", key);
    }
    return 0;
}
```

In this example:

- The linearSearch function takes an array, its size, and the key to search for.
- It uses a for loop to sequentially check each element in the array.
- If the key is found, the function returns its index; otherwise, it returns -1 to indicate that the key is not present.
- The main function demonstrates the usage by searching for a user-input element in the array and displaying the result.

Linear search has a time complexity of $O(n)$, where n is the size of the array. It is suitable for small-sized arrays or when the elements are not sorted.

2.3.Quadratic probing

Quadratic probing is a technique used in hash tables to resolve collisions. It involves using a quadratic function to determine the next probe location when a collision occurs. Here's an example of implementing quadratic probing in C:

```c
#include <stdio.h>
#include <stdlib.h>
#define SIZE 11 // Size of the hash table
// Hash table structure
struct HashTable
{
   int *array;
   int size;
};
// Function to initialize a hash table
struct HashTable* createHashTable(int size)
{
   struct HashTable* hashTable = (struct HashTable*)malloc(sizeof(struct HashTable));
   hashTable->array = (int*)malloc(size * sizeof(int));
   hashTable->size = size;
   // Initialize all elements in the hash table to -1 (indicating empty)
   for (int i = 0; i < size; i++)
   {
       hashTable->array[i] = -1;
   }
   return hashTable;
}
// Function to perform quadratic probing and insert a key into the hash table
void insertKey(struct HashTable* hashTable, int key)
{
   int index = key % hashTable->size; // Initial index using modulo
```

```c
    // Quadratic probing
    int i = 1;
    while (hashTable->array[index] != -1)
{

        index = (index + i * i) % hashTable->size;

        i++;

    }
    // Insert the key at the found index
    hashTable->array[index] = key;

}
// Function to display the contents of the hash table
void displayHashTable(struct HashTable* hashTable)
{

    printf("Hash Table: ");
    for (int i = 0; i < hashTable->size; i++)

{

        if (hashTable->array[i] != -1)

{

            printf("%d ", hashTable->array[i]);
        } else

{

            printf("- ");

        }

    }
    printf("\n");

}
int main()

{

    struct HashTable* hashTable = createHashTable(SIZE);
    // Insert keys into the hash table
```

```
    insertKey(hashTable, 12);
    insertKey(hashTable, 44);
    insertKey(hashTable, 13);
    insertKey(hashTable, 88);
    insertKey(hashTable, 23);
    insertKey(hashTable, 94);
    insertKey(hashTable, 11);
    insertKey(hashTable, 39);
    insertKey(hashTable, 20);
    // Display the contents of the hash table
    displayHashTable(hashTable);
    free(hashTable->array);
    free(hashTable);
    return 0;
}
```

In this example:

- The HashTable structure represents the hash table, and it contains an array and the size of the hash table.

- The createHashTable function initializes a hash table with all elements set to -1 (indicating empty).

- The insertKey function uses quadratic probing to find the next available slot in the hash table and inserts the key at that position.

- The displayHashTable function is used to print the contents of the hash table.

This is a simple demonstration of quadratic probing for educational purposes. In practical scenarios, more advanced techniques, such as double hashing or chaining, may be used to handle collisions in hash tables.

2.4. Linear Probing

Linear probing is a technique used in hash tables to resolve collisions. It involves probing consecutive locations in the hash table until an empty slot is found. Here's an example of implementing linear probing in C:

```c
#include <stdio.h>
#include <stdlib.h>
#define SIZE 11 // Size of the hash table
// Hash table structure
struct HashTable
{
   int *array;
   int size;
};
// Function to initialize a hash table
struct HashTable* createHashTable(int size)
{
   struct HashTable* hashTable = (struct HashTable*)malloc(sizeof(struct HashTable));
   hashTable->array = (int*)malloc(size * sizeof(int));
   hashTable->size = size;
   // Initialize all elements in the hash table to -1 (indicating empty)
   for (int i = 0; i < size; i++)
{
      hashTable->array[i] = -1;
   }
   return hashTable;
}
// Function to perform linear probing and insert a key into the hash table
void insertKey(struct HashTable* hashTable, int key)
{
   int index = key % hashTable->size; // Initial index using modulo
```

```c
    // Linear probing
    while (hashTable->array[index] != -1)
{

    index = (index + 1) % hashTable->size;

    }
    // Insert the key at the found index
    hashTable->array[index] = key;

}
// Function to display the contents of the hash table
void displayHashTable(struct HashTable* hashTable)

{

    printf("Hash Table: ");
    for (int i = 0; i < hashTable->size; i++)

{

    if (hashTable->array[i] != -1)

{

        printf("%d ", hashTable->array[i]);

    }
else

{

        printf("- ");

    }

    }
    printf("\n");

}
int main()

{

    struct HashTable* hashTable = createHashTable(SIZE);
    // Insert keys into the hash table
    insertKey(hashTable, 12);
```

```c
    insertKey(hashTable, 44);
    insertKey(hashTable, 13);
    insertKey(hashTable, 88);
    insertKey(hashTable, 23);
    insertKey(hashTable, 94);
    insertKey(hashTable, 11);
    insertKey(hashTable, 39);
    insertKey(hashTable, 20);
    // Display the contents of the hash table
    displayHashTable(hashTable);
    free(hashTable->array);
    free(hashTable);
    return 0;
}
```

In this example:

- The HashTable structure represents the hash table, and it contains an array and the size of the hash table.
- The createHashTable function initializes a hash table with all elements set to -1 (indicating empty).
- The insertKey function uses linear probing to find the next available slot in the hash table and inserts the key at that position.
- The displayHashTable function is used to print the contents of the hash table.

This is a simple demonstration of linear probing for educational purposes. In practical scenarios, more advanced techniques, such as double hashing or chaining, may be used to handle collisions in hash tables.

3.LINKED LIST

3.1. Create a linked list

```c
#include <stdio.h>
#include <stdlib.h>
// Define a node structure for the linked list
struct Node
{
    int data;
    struct Node* next;
};
// Function to create a new node
struct Node* createNode(int newData)
{
    struct Node* newNode = (struct Node*)malloc(sizeof(struct Node));
    if (newNode == NULL)
    {

        printf("Memory allocation failed.\n");
        exit(EXIT_FAILURE);
    }
    newNode->data = newData;
    newNode->next = NULL;
    return newNode;
}
// Function to insert a new node at the beginning of the linked list
void insertAtBeginning(struct Node** head, int newData)
{
    struct Node* newNode = createNode(newData);
    newNode->next = *head;
    *head = newNode;
}
```

```c
// Function to print the linked list
void printList(struct Node* node)
{
    while (node != NULL)
    {

        printf("%d -> ", node->data);
        node = node->next;
    }
    printf("NULL\n");
}
int main()
{
    // Initialize an empty linked list
    struct Node* head = NULL;
    // Insert nodes at the beginning
    insertAtBeginning(&head, 3);
    insertAtBeginning(&head, 8);
    insertAtBeginning(&head, 12);
    // Print the linked list
    printf("Linked List: ");
    printList(head);
    return 0;
}
```

In this example:

- The Node structure defines the structure of a node in the linked list, containing data and a pointer to the next node.
- The createNode function allocates memory for a new node and initializes its data and next pointers.
- The insertAtBeginning function inserts a new node at the beginning of the linked list.
- The printList function prints the elements of the linked list.

This program demonstrates creating a linked list with three nodes (containing data 12, 8, and 3) and then prints the linked list.

3.2. Perform insert operation

Below is an example of performing the insert operation in a singly linked list in C programming. The program includes functions to insert a node at the beginning, at the end, and at a specific position in the linked list:

```c
#include <stdio.h>
#include <stdlib.h>
// Define a node structure for the linked list
struct Node
{
    int data;
    struct Node* next;
};
// Function to create a new node
struct Node* createNode(int newData)
{
    struct Node* newNode = (struct Node*)malloc(sizeof(struct Node));
    if (newNode == NULL)
    {
        printf("Memory allocation failed.\n");
        exit(EXIT_FAILURE);
    }
    newNode->data = newData;
    newNode->next = NULL;
    return newNode;
}
// Function to insert a new node at the beginning of the linked list
void insertAtBeginning(struct Node** head, int newData)
{
    struct Node* newNode = createNode(newData);
    newNode->next = *head;
```

```c
    *head = newNode;
}
// Function to insert a new node at the end of the linked list
void insertAtEnd(struct Node** head, int newData)
{
    struct Node* newNode = createNode(newData);
    if (*head == NULL)
    {
        *head = newNode;
        return;
    }
    struct Node* temp = *head;
    while (temp->next != NULL)
    {
        temp = temp->next;
    }
    temp->next = newNode;
}
// Function to insert a new node at a specific position in the linked list
void insertAtPosition(struct Node** head, int newData, int position)
{
    if (position < 0)
    {
        printf("Invalid position for insertion.\n");
        return;
    }
    if (position == 0)
    {
        insertAtBeginning(head, newData);
        return;
```

```c
    }
    struct Node* newNode = createNode(newData);
    struct Node* temp = *head;
    for (int i = 1; i < position && temp != NULL; i++)
    {
        temp = temp->next;
    }
    if (temp == NULL)
    {
        printf("Invalid position for insertion.\n");
        return;
    }
    newNode->next = temp->next;
    temp->next = newNode;
}
// Function to print the linked list
void printList(struct Node* node)
{
    while (node != NULL)
    {
        printf("%d -> ", node->data);
        node = node->next;
    }
    printf("NULL\n");
}
int main()
{
    // Initialize an empty linked list
    struct Node* head = NULL;
```

```c
// Insert nodes at the beginning
insertAtBeginning(&head, 3);
insertAtBeginning(&head, 8);
insertAtBeginning(&head, 12);
// Print the linked list
printf("Linked List (after beginning insertions): ");
printList(head);
// Insert a node at the end
insertAtEnd(&head, 15);
// Print the linked list after end insertion
printf("Linked List (after end insertion): ");
printList(head);
// Insert a node at a specific position
insertAtPosition(&head, 5, 2);
// Print the linked list after position insertion
printf("Linked List (after position insertion): ");
printList(head);
return 0;
}
```

In this example, the insertAtBeginning, insertAtEnd, and insertAtPosition functions are used to insert nodes at the beginning, end, and a specific position in the linked list, respectively. The printList function is used to print the elements of the linked list.

3.3. Perform delete operation

Below is an example of performing the delete operation in a singly linked list in C programming. The program includes functions to delete a node from the beginning, end, and a specific position in the linked list:

```c
#include <stdio.h>
#include <stdlib.h>
// Define a node structure for the linked list
struct Node
{
   int data;
   struct Node* next;
};
// Function to create a new node
struct Node* createNode(int newData)
{
   struct Node* newNode = (struct Node*)malloc(sizeof(struct Node));
   if (newNode == NULL) {
     printf("Memory allocation failed.\n");
     exit(EXIT_FAILURE);
   }
   newNode->data = newData;
   newNode->next = NULL;
   return newNode;
}
// Function to insert a new node at the beginning of the linked list
void insertAtBeginning(struct Node** head, int newData)
{
   struct Node* newNode = createNode(newData);
   newNode->next = *head;
   *head = newNode;
```

```c
}
// Function to delete a node from the beginning of the linked list
void deleteFromBeginning(struct Node** head)
{
    if (*head == NULL)
    {
        printf("Linked list is empty. Nothing to delete.\n");
        return;
    }
    struct Node* temp = *head;
    *head = (*head)->next;
    free(temp);
}
// Function to delete a node from the end of the linked list
void deleteFromEnd(struct Node** head)
{
    if (*head == NULL)
    {
        printf("Linked list is empty. Nothing to delete.\n");
        return;
    }
    if ((*head)->next == NULL)
    {
        // If there is only one node, delete it
        free(*head);
        *head = NULL;
        return;
    }
    struct Node* temp = *head;
    struct Node* prev = NULL;
```

```c
    while (temp->next != NULL)
{

    prev = temp;

    temp = temp->next;

    }

    prev->next = NULL;

    free(temp);

}
// Function to delete a node from a specific position in the linked list
void deleteFromPosition(struct Node** head, int position)
{

  if (*head == NULL)

{

    printf("Linked list is empty. Nothing to delete.\n");

    return;

    }

  if (position < 0)

{

    printf("Invalid position for deletion.\n");

    return;

    }

  if (position == 0)

{

    // If deleting the first node

    struct Node* temp = *head;

    *head = (*head)->next;

    free(temp);

    return;

    }

  struct Node* temp = *head;
```

```c
    struct Node* prev = NULL;
    for (int i = 0; i < position && temp != NULL; i++)
{

    prev = temp;
    temp = temp->next;

  }
  if (temp == NULL)
{

    printf("Invalid position for deletion.\n");
    return;

  }
  prev->next = temp->next;
  free(temp);
}
// Function to print the linked list
void printList(struct Node* node)
{
  while (node != NULL)
{

    printf("%d -> ", node->data);
    node = node->next;

  }
  printf("NULL\n");
}
int main()
{
  // Initialize an empty linked list
  struct Node* head = NULL;
  // Insert nodes at the beginning
  insertAtBeginning(&head, 3);
```

```c
insertAtBeginning(&head, 8);
insertAtBeginning(&head, 12);
// Print the linked list
printf("Linked List (after beginning insertions): ");
printList(head);
// Delete a node from the beginning
deleteFromBeginning(&head);
// Print the linked list after beginning deletion
printf("Linked List (after beginning deletion): ");
printList(head);
// Delete a node from the end
deleteFromEnd(&head);
// Print the linked list after end deletion
printf("Linked List (after end deletion): ");
printList(head);
// Delete a node from a specific position
deleteFromPosition(&head, 1);
// Print the linked list after position deletion
printf("Linked List (after position deletion): ");
printList(head);
return 0;
}
```

In this example, the deleteFromBeginning, deleteFromEnd, and deleteFromPosition functions are used to delete nodes from the beginning, end, and a specific position in the linked list, respectively. The printList function is used to print the elements of the linked list.

3.4. Perform traversal

Traversal in a linked list involves visiting each node in the list and performing some operation. Below is an example of performing traversal in a singly linked list in C programming:

```c
#include <stdio.h>
#include <stdlib.h>
// Define a node structure for the linked list
struct Node
{
   int data;
   struct Node* next;
};
// Function to create a new node
struct Node* createNode(int newData)
{
   struct Node* newNode = (struct Node*)malloc(sizeof(struct Node));
   if (newNode == NULL) {
     printf("Memory allocation failed.\n");
     exit(EXIT_FAILURE);
   }
   newNode->data = newData;
   newNode->next = NULL;
   return newNode;
}
// Function to insert a new node at the beginning of the linked list
void insertAtBeginning(struct Node** head, int newData)
{
   struct Node* newNode = createNode(newData);
   newNode->next = *head;
   *head = newNode;
}
```

```c
// Function to perform traversal and print the linked list
void traverseLinkedList(struct Node* head)
{
    printf("Linked List: ");
    while (head != NULL)
{
        printf("%d -> ", head->data);
        head = head->next;
    }
    printf("NULL\n");
}
int main()
{
    // Initialize an empty linked list
    struct Node* head = NULL;
    // Insert nodes at the beginning
    insertAtBeginning(&head, 3);
    insertAtBeginning(&head, 8);
    insertAtBeginning(&head, 12);
    // Perform traversal and print the linked list
    traverseLinkedList(head);
    return 0;
}
```

In this example:

- The traverseLinkedList function is used to perform traversal and print the linked list.
- The insertAtBeginning function is used to insert nodes at the beginning of the linked list.
- The createNode function is used to create a new node.
- The main function demonstrates inserting nodes at the beginning and performing traversal to print the linked list.

Output

When you run this program, it will output:

Linked List: 12 -> 8 -> 3 -> NULL

This shows the traversal of the linked list, printing each node's data as it goes through the list.

3.5. Display the linked list

To display the linked list in C programming, you can use a traversal function to print each element of the list. Here's an example:

```c
#include <stdio.h>
#include <stdlib.h>
// Define a node structure for the linked list
struct Node
{
   int data;
   struct Node* next;
};
// Function to create a new node
struct Node* createNode(int newData)
{
   struct Node* newNode = (struct Node*)malloc(sizeof(struct Node));
   if (newNode == NULL)
{
      printf("Memory allocation failed.\n");
      exit(EXIT_FAILURE);
   }
   newNode->data = newData;
   newNode->next = NULL;
   return newNode;
}
// Function to insert a new node at the beginning of the linked list
void insertAtBeginning(struct Node** head, int newData)
{
   struct Node* newNode = createNode(newData);
   newNode->next = *head;
   *head = newNode;
```

```c
}
// Function to display the linked list
void displayLinkedList(struct Node* head)
{
    printf("Linked List: ");
    while (head != NULL)
{
        printf("%d -> ", head->data);
        head = head->next;
    }
    printf("NULL\n");
}
int main()
{
    // Initialize an empty linked list
    struct Node* head = NULL;
    // Insert nodes at the beginning
    insertAtBeginning(&head, 3);
    insertAtBeginning(&head, 8);
    insertAtBeginning(&head, 12);
    // Display the linked list
    displayLinkedList(head);
    return 0;
}
```

In this example:

- The displayLinkedList function is used to display the linked list by traversing it and printing each element.
- The insertAtBeginning function is used to insert nodes at the beginning of the linked list.
- The createNode function is used to create a new node.

- The main function demonstrates inserting nodes at the beginning and displaying the linked list.

Output

When you run this program, it will output:

Linked List: 12 -> 8 -> 3 -> NULL

This shows the elements of the linked list in order. You can modify and extend these functions based on your specific requirements.

3.6. Implement a singly linked list

```c
#include <stdio.h>
#include <stdlib.h>
// Define a node structure for the linked list
struct Node
{
   int data;
   struct Node* next;
};


// Function to insert a new node at the beginning of the linked list
void insertAtBeginning(struct Node** head, int newData)
{
   // Allocate memory for a new node
   struct Node* newNode = (struct Node*)malloc(sizeof(struct Node));
   // Set data and link of the new node
   newNode->data = newData;
   newNode->next = *head;
   // Update the head to point to the new node
   *head = newNode;
}
// Function to print the linked list
void printList(struct Node* node)
{
   while (node != NULL) {
      printf("%d -> ", node->data);
      node = node->next;
   }
   printf("NULL\n");
}
```

```c
int main()
{
    // Initialize an empty linked list
    struct Node* head = NULL;
    // Insert nodes at the beginning
    insertAtBeginning(&head, 3);
    insertAtBeginning(&head, 8);
    insertAtBeginning(&head, 12);
    // Print the linked list
    printf("Linked List: ");
    printList(head);
    return 0;
}
```

Output

Linked List: 12 -> 8 -> 3 -> NULL

This program defines a basic singly linked list structure, provides a function to insert nodes at the beginning, and demonstrates inserting three nodes into the linked list. The printList function is then used to display the elements of the linked list.

3.7. Implement a doubly linked list

A doubly linked list is a type of linked list in which each node contains a data element and two pointers - one pointing to the next node and another pointing to the previous node. Here's an example of implementing a doubly linked list in C:

```c
#include <stdio.h>
#include <stdlib.h>
// Define a node structure for the doubly linked list
struct Node
{
   int data;
   struct Node* next;
   struct Node* prev;
};
// Function to create a new node
struct Node* createNode(int newData)
{
   struct Node* newNode = (struct Node*)malloc(sizeof(struct Node));
   if (newNode == NULL)
{
     printf("Memory allocation failed.\n");
     exit(EXIT_FAILURE);
   }
   newNode->data = newData;
   newNode->next = NULL;
   newNode->prev = NULL;
   return newNode;
}
// Function to insert a new node at the beginning of the doubly linked list
void insertAtBeginning(struct Node** head, int newData)
{
```

```c
    struct Node* newNode = createNode(newData);
    if (*head != NULL)
    {
        (*head)->prev = newNode;
    }
    newNode->next = *head;
    *head = newNode;
}
// Function to display the doubly linked list from the beginning
void displayForward(struct Node* head)
{
    printf("Doubly Linked List (Forward): ");
    while (head != NULL)
    {
        printf("%d <-> ", head->data);
        head = head->next;
    }
    printf("NULL\n");
}
// Function to display the doubly linked list from the end
void displayBackward(struct Node* tail)
{
    printf("Doubly Linked List (Backward): ");
    while (tail != NULL)
    {
        printf("%d <-> ", tail->data);
        tail = tail->prev;
    }
    printf("NULL\n");
}
```

```c
int main()
{
    // Initialize an empty doubly linked list
    struct Node* head = NULL;
    // Insert nodes at the beginning
    insertAtBeginning(&head, 3);
    insertAtBeginning(&head, 8);
    insertAtBeginning(&head, 12);
    // Display the doubly linked list from the beginning
    displayForward(head);
    // Display the doubly linked list from the end
    displayBackward(head);
    return 0;
}
```

In this example:

- The Node structure defines the structure of a node in the doubly linked list, containing data, a pointer to the next node, and a pointer to the previous node.
- The createNode function allocates memory for a new node and initializes its data and pointers.
- The insertAtBeginning function inserts a new node at the beginning of the doubly linked list.
- The displayForward function displays the doubly linked list from the beginning.
- The displayBackward function displays the doubly linked list from the end.

Output

When you run this program, it will output:

Doubly Linked List (Forward): 12 <-> 8 <-> 3 <-> NULL

Doubly Linked List (Backward): 3 <-> 8 <-> 12 <-> NULL

This shows the elements of the doubly linked list in both forward and backward directions.

3.8.Reverse a linked list

To reverse a linked list in C programming, you can iterate through the list, changing the direction of the pointers. Here's an example:

```c
#include <stdio.h>
#include <stdlib.h>
// Define a node structure for the linked list
struct Node
{
   int data;
   struct Node* next;
};
// Function to create a new node
struct Node* createNode(int newData)
{
   struct Node* newNode = (struct Node*)malloc(sizeof(struct Node));
   if (newNode == NULL)
{
      printf("Memory allocation failed.\n");
      exit(EXIT_FAILURE);
   }
   newNode->data = newData;
   newNode->next = NULL;
   return newNode;
}
// Function to insert a new node at the beginning of the linked list
void insertAtBeginning(struct Node** head, int newData)
{
   struct Node* newNode = createNode(newData);
   newNode->next = *head;
   *head = newNode;
```

```c
}
// Function to display the linked list
void displayList(struct Node* head)
{
    printf("Linked List: ");
    while (head != NULL)
    {
        printf("%d -> ", head->data);
        head = head->next;
    }
    printf("NULL\n");
}
// Function to reverse the linked list
void reverseList(struct Node** head)
{
    struct Node* current = *head;
    struct Node* prev = NULL;
    struct Node* nextNode = NULL;
    while (current != NULL)
    {
        nextNode = current->next; // Save the next node
        current->next = prev;     // Reverse the link
        prev = current;           // Move one step forward
        current = nextNode;       // Move one step forward
    }
    *head = prev; // Update the head to the last node (new first node)
}
int main()
{
    // Initialize an empty linked list
```

```c
struct Node* head = NULL;
// Insert nodes at the beginning
insertAtBeginning(&head, 3);
insertAtBeginning(&head, 8);
insertAtBeginning(&head, 12);
// Display the original linked list
printf("Original ");
displayList(head);
// Reverse the linked list
reverseList(&head);
// Display the reversed linked list
printf("Reversed ");
displayList(head);
return 0;
}
```

In this example:

- The reverseList function reverses the linked list by iterating through the list and changing the direction of the pointers.
- The insertAtBeginning function inserts nodes at the beginning of the linked list.
- The createNode function creates a new node.
- The displayList function displays the elements of the linked list.

Output

When you run this program, it will output:

Original Linked List: 12 -> 8 -> 3 -> NULL

Reversed Linked List: 3 -> 8 -> 12 -> NULL

This shows the original and reversed forms of the linked list.

3.9.Detecting loop in a linked list

Detecting a loop in a linked list can be done using Floyd's cycle-finding algorithm, also known as the "tortoise and hare" algorithm. This algorithm uses two pointers moving at different speeds to determine if there's a loop in the linked list. Here's an example of how you can implement loop detection in a linked list in C:

```c
#include <stdio.h>
#include <stdlib.h>
// Define a node structure for the linked list
struct Node
{
   int data;
   struct Node* next;
};
// Function to create a new node
struct Node* createNode(int newData)
{
   struct Node* newNode = (struct Node*)malloc(sizeof(struct Node));
   if (newNode == NULL)
{
      printf("Memory allocation failed.\n");
      exit(EXIT_FAILURE);
   }
   newNode->data = newData;
   newNode->next = NULL;
   return newNode;
}
// Function to insert a new node at the beginning of the linked list
void insertAtBeginning(struct Node** head, int newData)
{
   struct Node* newNode = createNode(newData);
```

```c
    newNode->next = *head;
    *head = newNode;
}
// Function to detect a loop in the linked list
int detectLoop(struct Node* head)
{
    struct Node* slow = head;
    struct Node* fast = head;
    while (fast != NULL && fast->next != NULL)
    {
        slow = slow->next;
        fast = fast->next->next;
        if (slow == fast)
        {
            // Loop detected
            return 1;
        }
    }
    // No loop
    return 0;
}
int main()
{
    // Initialize a linked list without a loop
    struct Node* headNoLoop = NULL;
    insertAtBeginning(&headNoLoop, 3);
    insertAtBeginning(&headNoLoop, 8);
    insertAtBeginning(&headNoLoop, 12);
    // Detect loop in the linked list without a loop
    if (detectLoop(headNoLoop))
```

```c
{
    printf("Loop detected in the linked list without a loop.\n");
} else
{
    printf("No loop detected in the linked list without a loop.\n");
}
// Create a linked list with a loop
struct Node* headWithLoop = NULL;
insertAtBeginning(&headWithLoop, 3);
insertAtBeginning(&headWithLoop, 8);
insertAtBeginning(&headWithLoop, 12);
// Creating a loop (connecting the last node to the second node)
headWithLoop->next->next->next = headWithLoop->next;
// Detect loop in the linked list with a loop
if (detectLoop(headWithLoop))
{
    printf("Loop detected in the linked list with a loop.\n");
} else
{
    printf("No loop detected in the linked list with a loop.\n");
}
return 0;
}
```

In this example:

- The detectLoop function uses the "tortoise and hare" algorithm to detect a loop in the linked list.
- The insertAtBeginning function inserts nodes at the beginning of the linked list.
- The createNode function creates a new node.
- The main function demonstrates detecting a loop in a linked list without a loop and with a loop.

Output

When you run this program, it will output:

No loop detected in the linked list without a loop.

Loop detected in the linked list with a loop.

This shows the results of detecting loops in linked lists.

3.10. Removing loops in a linked list.

To remove a loop in a linked list, you can modify the Floyd's cycle-finding algorithm to identify the node where the loop starts. Once the loop-starting node is identified, you can break the loop by setting the next pointer of the last node in the loop to NULL. Here's an example of how to remove a loop from a linked list in C:

```c
#include <stdio.h>
#include <stdlib.h>
// Define a node structure for the linked list
struct Node
{
   int data;
   struct Node* next;
};
// Function to create a new node
struct Node* createNode(int newData)
{
   struct Node* newNode = (struct Node*)malloc(sizeof(struct Node));
   if (newNode == NULL)
{
      printf("Memory allocation failed.\n");
      exit(EXIT_FAILURE);
   }
   newNode->data = newData;
   newNode->next = NULL;
   return newNode;
}
// Function to insert a new node at the beginning of the linked list
void insertAtBeginning(struct Node** head, int newData)
{
   struct Node* newNode = createNode(newData);
```

```c
    newNode->next = *head;

    *head = newNode;

}
// Function to detect and remove a loop in the linked list
void detectAndRemoveLoop(struct Node* head)

{

    struct Node* slow = head;

    struct Node* fast = head;

    // Detect loop using Floyd's cycle-finding algorithm

    while (fast != NULL && fast->next != NULL)

    {

        slow = slow->next;

        fast = fast->next->next;

        if (slow == fast)

        {

            // Loop detected, remove the loop

            removeLoop(head, slow);

            return;

        }

    }

}
// Function to remove a loop in the linked list
void removeLoop(struct Node* head, struct Node* loopNode)

{

    struct Node* ptr1 = head;

    struct Node* ptr2 = loopNode;

    // Move ptr1 to the head, and move both pointers one node at a time

    // until they meet at the start of the loop

    while (ptr1->next != ptr2->next)

    {
```

```c
        ptr1 = ptr1->next;
        ptr2 = ptr2->next;
    }
    // Set the next pointer of the last node in the loop to NULL
    ptr2->next = NULL;
}
// Function to display the linked list
void displayList(struct Node* head)
{
    printf("Linked List: ");
    while (head != NULL)
    {
        printf("%d -> ", head->data);
        head = head->next;
    }
    printf("NULL\n");
}
int main()
{
    // Initialize a linked list without a loop
    struct Node* headNoLoop = NULL;
    insertAtBeginning(&headNoLoop, 3);
    insertAtBeginning(&headNoLoop, 8);
    insertAtBeginning(&headNoLoop, 12);
    // Detect and remove loop in the linked list without a loop
    detectAndRemoveLoop(headNoLoop);
    // Display the linked list without a loop
    displayList(headNoLoop);
    // Create a linked list with a loop
    struct Node* headWithLoop = NULL;
```

```
insertAtBeginning(&headWithLoop, 3);
insertAtBeginning(&headWithLoop, 8);
insertAtBeginning(&headWithLoop, 12);
// Creating a loop (connecting the last node to the second node)
headWithLoop->next->next->next = headWithLoop->next;
// Detect and remove loop in the linked list with a loop
detectAndRemoveLoop(headWithLoop);
// Display the linked list after removing the loop
displayList(headWithLoop);
return 0;
}
```

In this example:

- The detectAndRemoveLoop function uses the Floyd's cycle-finding algorithm to detect a loop in the linked list and calls removeLoop to remove it.
- The removeLoop function identifies the start of the loop and sets the next pointer of the last node in the loop to NULL.
- The insertAtBeginning function inserts nodes at the beginning of the linked list.
- The createNode function creates a new node.
- The displayList function displays the elements of the linked list.

Output

When you run this program, it will output:

Linked List without a loop: 12 -> 8 -> 3 -> NULL

Linked List after removing the loop: 12 -> 8 -> 3 -> NULL

This demonstrates the removal of a loop from a linked list.

4. SORTING

4.1. Bubble sort

Bubble Sort is a simple sorting algorithm that repeatedly steps through the list, compares adjacent elements, and swaps them if they are in the wrong order. The pass through the list is repeated until the list is sorted. Below is an example of implementing Bubble Sort in C:

```c
#include <stdio.h>
// Function to perform Bubble Sort
void bubbleSort(int arr[], int n)
{
  for (int i = 0; i < n - 1; i++)
{
    for (int j = 0; j < n - i - 1; j++)
{
      // Swap if the element found is greater than the next element
      if (arr[j] > arr[j + 1])
{
        int temp = arr[j];
        arr[j] = arr[j + 1];
        arr[j + 1] = temp;
      }
    }
  }
}
// Function to print an array
void printArray(int arr[], int size)
{
  for (int i = 0; i < size; i++)
{
    printf("%d ", arr[i]);
  }
```

```c
    printf("\n");
}
int main()
{
    int arr[] = {64, 34, 25, 12, 22, 11, 90};
    int n = sizeof(arr) / sizeof(arr[0]);
    printf("Original array: ");
    printArray(arr, n);
    // Perform Bubble Sort
    bubbleSort(arr, n);
    printf("Sorted array: ");
    printArray(arr, n);
    return 0;
}
```

In this example:

- The bubbleSort function implements the Bubble Sort algorithm.
- The printArray function is used to print the elements of an array.
- The main function initializes an array, prints the original array, performs Bubble Sort, and then prints the sorted array.

Output

When you run this program, it will output:

Original array: 64 34 25 12 22 11 90

Sorted array: 11 12 22 25 34 64 90

This shows the array before and after the Bubble Sort operation. Note that Bubble Sort is not the most efficient sorting algorithm for large datasets, but it's simple to understand and implement. Other more efficient sorting algorithms like Quick Sort or Merge Sort are often preferred for larger datasets.

4.2.Selection sort

Selection Sort is a simple sorting algorithm that works by repeatedly finding the minimum element from the unsorted part of the array and putting it at the beginning. Here's an example of implementing Selection Sort in C:

```c
#include <stdio.h>
// Function to perform Selection Sort
void selectionSort(int arr[], int n)
{
  for (int i = 0; i < n - 1; i++)
  {
      // Find the minimum element in the unsorted part
      int minIndex = i;
      for (int j = i + 1; j < n; j++)
      {
          if (arr[j] < arr[minIndex])
          {
              minIndex = j;
          }
      }
      // Swap the found minimum element with the first element
      int temp = arr[i];
      arr[i] = arr[minIndex];
      arr[minIndex] = temp;
  }
}
// Function to print an array
void printArray(int arr[], int size)
{
  for (int i = 0; i < size; i++)
  {
```

```c
        printf("%d ", arr[i]);
    }
    printf("\n");
}
int main()
{
    int arr[] = {64, 34, 25, 12, 22, 11, 90};
    int n = sizeof(arr) / sizeof(arr[0]);
    printf("Original array: ");
    printArray(arr, n);
    // Perform Selection Sort
    selectionSort(arr, n);
    printf("Sorted array: ");
    printArray(arr, n);
    return 0;
}
```

In this example:

- The selectionSort function implements the Selection Sort algorithm.
- The printArray function is used to print the elements of an array.
- The main function initializes an array, prints the original array, performs Selection Sort, and then prints the sorted array.

Output

When you run this program, it will output:

Original array: 64 34 25 12 22 11 90

Sorted array: 11 12 22 25 34 64 90

This shows the array before and after the Selection Sort operation. Similar to Bubble Sort, Selection Sort is not the most efficient sorting algorithm for large datasets, but it's simple to understand and implement. Other more efficient sorting algorithms like Quick Sort or Merge Sort are often preferred for larger datasets.

4.3. Insertion sort

Insertion Sort is a simple sorting algorithm that builds the final sorted array one item at a time. It is much less efficient on large lists than more advanced algorithms such as quicksort, heapsort, or merge sort. However, it has the advantage of a simple implementation and is efficient for small data sets. Here's an example of implementing Insertion Sort in C:

```c
#include <stdio.h>
// Function to perform Insertion Sort
void insertionSort(int arr[], int n)
{
    for (int i = 1; i < n; i++)
    {
        int key = arr[i];
        int j = i - 1;
        // Move elements of arr[0..i-1] that are greater than key to one position ahead of their current position
        while (j >= 0 && arr[j] > key)
        {
            arr[j + 1] = arr[j];
            j = j - 1;
        }
        arr[j + 1] = key;
    }
}
// Function to print an array
void printArray(int arr[], int size)
{
    for (int i = 0; i < size; i++)
    {
        printf("%d ", arr[i]);
    }
```

```c
    printf("\n");
}
int main()
{
    int arr[] = {64, 34, 25, 12, 22, 11, 90};
    int n = sizeof(arr) / sizeof(arr[0]);
    printf("Original array: ");
    printArray(arr, n);
    // Perform Insertion Sort
    insertionSort(arr, n);
    printf("Sorted array: ");
    printArray(arr, n);
    return 0;
}
```

In this example:

- The insertionSort function implements the Insertion Sort algorithm.
- The printArray function is used to print the elements of an array.
- The main function initializes an array, prints the original array, performs Insertion Sort, and then prints the sorted array.

Output

When you run this program, it will output:

Original array: 64 34 25 12 22 11 90

Sorted array: 11 12 22 25 34 64 90

This shows the array before and after the Insertion Sort operation. Insertion Sort is often efficient for small data sets or nearly sorted data. For larger datasets, other more advanced sorting algorithms may be preferred.

4.4. Merge sort

Merge Sort is a divide-and-conquer algorithm that divides the unsorted list into n sublists, each containing one element, and then repeatedly merges sublists to produce new sorted sublists until there is only one sublist remaining. Here's an example of implementing Merge Sort in C:

```c
#include <stdio.h>
#include <stdlib.h>
// Function to merge two subarrays of arr[]
void merge(int arr[], int left, int middle, int right)
{
    int i, j, k;
    int n1 = middle - left + 1;
    int n2 = right - middle;
    // Create temporary arrays
    int L[n1], R[n2];
    // Copy data to temporary arrays L[] and R[]
    for (i = 0; i < n1; i++)
        L[i] = arr[left + i];
    for (j = 0; j < n2; j++)
        R[j] = arr[middle + 1 + j];
    // Merge the temporary arrays back into arr[left..right]
    i = 0; // Initial index of first subarray
    j = 0; // Initial index of second subarray
    k = left; // Initial index of merged subarray
    while (i < n1 && j < n2)
    {
        if (L[i] <= R[j])
        {
            arr[k] = L[i];
            i++;
        }
```

```c
else
{
        arr[k] = R[j];
        j++;
}
    k++;
  }
  // Copy the remaining elements of L[], if there are any
  while (i < n1)
{
    arr[k] = L[i];
    i++;
    k++;
  }
  // Copy the remaining elements of R[], if there are any
  while (j < n2)
{
    arr[k] = R[j];
    j++;
    k++;
  }
}
// Function to perform Merge Sort
void mergeSort(int arr[], int left, int right)
{
  if (left < right)
{
      // Same as (left+right)/2, but avoids overflow for large left and right
      int middle = left + (right - left) / 2;
      // Sort first and second halves
```

```c
        mergeSort(arr, left, middle);
        mergeSort(arr, middle + 1, right);
        // Merge the sorted halves
        merge(arr, left, middle, right);
    }
}
// Function to print an array
void printArray(int arr[], int size)
{
    for (int i = 0; i < size; i++)
    {
        printf("%d ", arr[i]);
    }
    printf("\n");
}
int main()
{
    int arr[] = {64, 34, 25, 12, 22, 11, 90};
    int n = sizeof(arr) / sizeof(arr[0]);
    printf("Original array: ");
    printArray(arr, n);
    // Perform Merge Sort
    mergeSort(arr, 0, n - 1);
    printf("Sorted array: ");
    printArray(arr, n);
    return 0;
}
```

In this example:

- The merge function merges two sorted subarrays into one.
- The mergeSort function implements the Merge Sort algorithm.

- The printArray function is used to print the elements of an array.
- The main function initializes an array, prints the original array, performs Merge Sort, and then prints the sorted array.

Output

When you run this program, it will output:

Original array: 64 34 25 12 22 11 90

Sorted array: 11 12 22 25 34 64 90

This shows the array before and after the Merge Sort operation. Merge Sort is a more efficient sorting algorithm compared to Bubble Sort or Selection Sort, especially for larger datasets.

4.5.Quick sort

Quick Sort is a divide-and-conquer sorting algorithm that works by selecting a 'pivot' element from the array and partitioning the other elements into two sub-arrays according to whether they are less than or greater than the pivot. The sub-arrays are then sorted recursively. Here's an example of implementing Quick Sort in C:

```c
#include <stdio.h>
// Function to swap two elements in an array
void swap(int* a, int* b)
{
    int temp = *a;
    *a = *b;
    *b = temp;
}
// Function to partition the array and return the pivot index
int partition(int arr[], int low, int high)
{
    int pivot = arr[high]; // Choose the last element as the pivot
    int i = low - 1; // Index of smaller element
    for (int j = low; j <= high - 1; j++)
    {
        // If the current element is smaller than or equal to the pivot
        if (arr[j] <= pivot)
        {
            i++;
            swap(&arr[i], &arr[j]);
        }
    }
    // Swap the pivot element with the element at (i + 1), so that
    // the pivot is now at its correct sorted position
    swap(&arr[i + 1], &arr[high]);
```

```c
    return i + 1; // Return the pivot index
}
// Function to perform Quick Sort
void quickSort(int arr[], int low, int high)
{
    if (low < high)
    {
        // Find the pivot index such that elements smaller than the pivot are on the left
        // and elements greater than the pivot are on the right
        int pivotIndex = partition(arr, low, high);
        // Recursively sort the subarrays
        quickSort(arr, low, pivotIndex - 1);
        quickSort(arr, pivotIndex + 1, high);
    }
}
// Function to print an array
void printArray(int arr[], int size)
{
    for (int i = 0; i < size; i++)
    {
        printf("%d ", arr[i]);
    }
    printf("\n");
}
int main()
{
    int arr[] = {64, 34, 25, 12, 22, 11, 90};
    int n = sizeof(arr) / sizeof(arr[0]);
    printf("Original array: ");
    printArray(arr, n);
```

```
// Perform Quick Sort
quickSort(arr, 0, n - 1);
printf("Sorted array: ");
printArray(arr, n);
return 0;
}
```

In this example:

- The swap function is used to swap two elements in an array.
- The partition function chooses the last element as the pivot, rearranges the array so that elements smaller than the pivot are on the left, and elements greater than the pivot are on the right. It returns the pivot index.
- The quickSort function implements the Quick Sort algorithm by recursively sorting subarrays.
- The printArray function is used to print the elements of an array.
- The main function initializes an array, prints the original array, performs Quick Sort, and then prints the sorted array.

Output

When you run this program, it will output:

Original array: 64 34 25 12 22 11 90

Sorted array: 11 12 22 25 34 64 90

This shows the array before and after the Quick Sort operation. Quick Sort is a widely used sorting algorithm known for its efficiency, especially for large datasets.

4.6. Topological sort

Topological sorting is an ordering of the nodes in a directed acyclic graph (DAG) such that for every directed edge (u, v), node u comes before node v in the ordering. It is used in various applications, including task scheduling and dependency resolution. Below is an example of implementing topological sort in C using depth-first search (DFS):

```c
#include <stdio.h>
#include <stdlib.h>
// Define the maximum number of vertices in the graph
#define MAX_VERTICES 100
// Structure for representing a graph
struct Graph
{
    int numVertices;
    int** adjacencyMatrix;
};
// Structure for representing a stack
struct Stack
{
    int top;
    int capacity;
    int* array;
};
// Function to create a new stack
struct Stack* createStack(int capacity)
{
    struct Stack* stack = (struct Stack*)malloc(sizeof(struct Stack));
    stack->top = -1;
    stack->capacity = capacity;
    stack->array = (int*)malloc(stack->capacity * sizeof(int));
    return stack;
```

```c
}
// Function to check if the stack is empty
int isEmpty(struct Stack* stack)
{
    return stack->top == -1;
}
// Function to push an element onto the stack
void push(struct Stack* stack, int item)
{
    stack->array[++stack->top] = item;
}
// Function to pop an element from the stack
int pop(struct Stack* stack)
{
    if (isEmpty(stack))
        return -1;
    return stack->array[stack->top--];
}
// Function to initialize a graph with a given number of vertices
struct Graph* createGraph(int numVertices)
{
    struct Graph* graph = (struct Graph*)malloc(sizeof(struct Graph));
    graph->numVertices = numVertices;
    // Allocate memory for the adjacency matrix
    graph->adjacencyMatrix = (int**)malloc(numVertices * sizeof(int*));
    for (int i = 0; i < numVertices; i++)
    {
        graph->adjacencyMatrix[i] = (int*)malloc(numVertices * sizeof(int));
        for (int j = 0; j < numVertices; j++)
            graph->adjacencyMatrix[i][j] = 0;
```

```c
    }
    return graph;
}
// Function to add an edge to the graph
void addEdge(struct Graph* graph, int startVertex, int endVertex)
{
    graph->adjacencyMatrix[startVertex][endVertex] = 1;
}
// Function to perform depth-first search (DFS) and perform topological sorting
void topologicalSortUtil(struct Graph* graph, int vertex, int visited[], struct Stack* stack)
{
    visited[vertex] = 1;
    // Recur for all the vertices adjacent to this vertex
    for (int i = 0; i < graph->numVertices; i++)
    {
        if (graph->adjacencyMatrix[vertex][i] && !visited[i])
            topologicalSortUtil(graph, i, visited, stack);
    }
    // Push current vertex to stack, which will be the topological order
    push(stack, vertex);
}
// Function to perform topological sort on a directed acyclic graph (DAG)
void topologicalSort(struct Graph* graph)
{
    struct Stack* stack = createStack(graph->numVertices);
    int* visited = (int*)malloc(graph->numVertices * sizeof(int));
    for (int i = 0; i < graph->numVertices; i++)
        visited[i] = 0;
    // Perform DFS and push vertices to stack
    for (int i = 0; i < graph->numVertices; i++)
```

```c
{
      if (!visited[i])
          topologicalSortUtil(graph, i, visited, stack);
    }
    // Print the topological order
    printf("Topological Order: ");
    while (!isEmpty(stack))
       printf("%d ", pop(stack));
    printf("\n");
    // Free allocated memory
    free(stack->array);
    free(stack);
    free(visited);
}
int main()
{
    int numVertices = 6;
    struct Graph* graph = createGraph(numVertices);
    // Add edges to the graph
    addEdge(graph, 5, 2);
    addEdge(graph, 5, 0);
    addEdge(graph, 4, 0);
    addEdge(graph, 4, 1);
    addEdge(graph, 2, 3);
    addEdge(graph, 3, 1);
    // Perform topological sort
    topologicalSort(graph);
    // Free allocated memory
    for (int i = 0; i < numVertices; i++)
       free(graph->adjacencyMatrix[i]);
```

```
free(graph->adjacencyMatrix);
free(graph);
return 0;
}
```

In this example:

- The Graph structure represents a directed graph using an adjacency matrix.
- The Stack structure is used to implement a stack for topological sorting.
- The createStack, isEmpty, push, and pop functions are for stack operations.
- The createGraph, addEdge, and topologicalSort functions are used to create a graph, add edges, and perform topological sort.
- The topologicalSortUtil function is a utility function for DFS and topological sorting.

Output

When you run this program, it will output:

Topological Order: 5 4 2 3 1 0

This shows the topological order of the nodes in the directed acyclic graph (DAG).

5.STACK

5.1. Implement a stack using arrays (Push and pop operations)

Below is a simple implementation of a stack using arrays in C, with push and pop operations:

```c
#include <stdio.h>
#include <stdlib.h>
#define MAX_SIZE 100
// Structure to represent a stack
struct Stack
{
  int top;
  int array[MAX_SIZE];
};
// Function to initialize a stack
struct Stack* createStack()
{
  struct Stack* stack = (struct Stack*)malloc(sizeof(struct Stack));
  stack->top = -1;
  return stack;
}
// Function to check if the stack is empty
int isEmpty(struct Stack* stack)
{
  return stack->top == -1;
}
// Function to check if the stack is full
int isFull(struct Stack* stack)
{
  return stack->top == MAX_SIZE - 1;
}
```

```c
// Function to push an element onto the stack
void push(struct Stack* stack, int item)
{
    if (isFull(stack))
    {
        printf("Stack overflow: Cannot push %d, stack is full.\n", item);
        return;
    }
    stack->array[++stack->top] = item;
    printf("%d pushed to stack.\n", item);
}
// Function to pop an element from the stack
int pop(struct Stack* stack)
{
    if (isEmpty(stack))
    {
        printf("Stack underflow: Cannot pop from an empty stack.\n");
        return -1; // Return an invalid value
    }
    return stack->array[stack->top--];
}
// Function to get the top element of the stack without popping
int peek(struct Stack* stack)
{
    if (isEmpty(stack))
    {
        printf("Stack is empty.\n");
        return -1; // Return an invalid value
    }
    return stack->array[stack->top];
```

```c
}
// Function to print the elements of the stack
void printStack(struct Stack* stack)
{
   if (isEmpty(stack))
   {
      printf("Stack is empty.\n");
      return;
   }
   printf("Stack elements: ");
   for (int i = 0; i <= stack->top; i++)
   {
      printf("%d ", stack->array[i]);
   }
   printf("\n");
}
int main()
{
   // Create a stack
   struct Stack* stack = createStack();
   // Push elements onto the stack
   push(stack, 10);
   push(stack, 20);
   push(stack, 30);
   // Print the stack
   printStack(stack);
   // Get and print the top element without popping
   printf("Top element: %d\n", peek(stack));
   // Pop elements from the stack
   printf("Popped element: %d\n", pop(stack));
```

```c
printf("Popped element: %d\n", pop(stack));
// Print the updated stack
printStack(stack);
return 0;
}
```

In this example:

- The Stack structure represents a stack with an array.
- The createStack, isEmpty, isFull, push, pop, peek, and printStack functions are used to perform stack operations.
- The main function demonstrates creating a stack, pushing elements onto the stack, popping elements from the stack, getting the top element without popping, and printing the stack.

Output

When you run this program, it will output:

```
10 pushed to stack.
20 pushed to stack.
30 pushed to stack.
Stack elements: 10 20 30
Top element: 30
Popped element: 30
Popped element: 20
Stack elements: 10
```

This demonstrates the basic operations of a stack using arrays in C.

5.2. Implement a stack using linked lists (Push and pop operations)

Below is a simple implementation of a stack using linked lists in C, with push and pop operations:

```c
#include <stdio.h>
#include <stdlib.h>
// Structure to represent a node in the linked list
struct Node
{
   int data;
   struct Node* next;
};
// Structure to represent a stack
struct Stack
{
   struct Node* top;
};
// Function to initialize a stack
struct Stack* createStack()
{
   struct Stack* stack = (struct Stack*)malloc(sizeof(struct Stack));
   stack->top = NULL;
   return stack;
}
// Function to check if the stack is empty
int isEmpty(struct Stack* stack)
{
   return stack->top == NULL;
}
// Function to create a new node with the given data
struct Node* createNode(int data)
```

```c
{
    struct Node* newNode = (struct Node*)malloc(sizeof(struct Node));
    newNode->data = data;
    newNode->next = NULL;
    return newNode;
}
// Function to push an element onto the stack
void push(struct Stack* stack, int item)
{
    struct Node* newNode = createNode(item);
    newNode->next = stack->top;
    stack->top = newNode;
    printf("%d pushed to stack.\n", item);
}
// Function to pop an element from the stack
int pop(struct Stack* stack)
{
    if (isEmpty(stack))
    {
        printf("Stack underflow: Cannot pop from an empty stack.\n");
        return -1; // Return an invalid value
    }
    struct Node* poppedNode = stack->top;
    int poppedData = poppedNode->data;
    stack->top = poppedNode->next;
    free(poppedNode);
    printf("%d popped from stack.\n", poppedData);
    return poppedData;
}
```

```c
// Function to get the top element of the stack without popping
int peek(struct Stack* stack)
{
   if (isEmpty(stack))
   {
      printf("Stack is empty.\n");
      return -1; // Return an invalid value
   }
   return stack->top->data;
}
// Function to print the elements of the stack
void printStack(struct Stack* stack)
{
   if (isEmpty(stack))
   {
      printf("Stack is empty.\n");
      return;
   }
   printf("Stack elements: ");
   struct Node* current = stack->top;
   while (current != NULL)
   {
      printf("%d ", current->data);
      current = current->next;
   }
   printf("\n");
}
// Function to free the memory allocated for the stack
void freeStack(struct Stack* stack)
{
```

```c
    while (!isEmpty(stack))
{
    pop(stack);
  }
    free(stack);
}
int main()
{
    // Create a stack
    struct Stack* stack = createStack();
    // Push elements onto the stack
    push(stack, 10);
    push(stack, 20);
    push(stack, 30);
    // Print the stack
    printStack(stack);
    // Get and print the top element without popping
    printf("Top element: %d\n", peek(stack));
    // Pop elements from the stack
    printf("Popped element: %d\n", pop(stack));
    printf("Popped element: %d\n", pop(stack));
    // Print the updated stack
    printStack(stack);
    // Free the memory allocated for the stack
    freeStack(stack);
    return 0;
}
```

In this example:

- The Node structure represents a node in the linked list.
- The Stack structure represents a stack using a linked list.

- The createStack, isEmpty, createNode, push, pop, peek, printStack, and freeStack functions are used to perform stack operations.

- The main function demonstrates creating a stack, pushing elements onto the stack, popping elements from the stack, getting the top element without popping, and printing the stack.

Output

When you run this program, it will output:

10 pushed to stack.

20 pushed to stack.

30 pushed to stack.

Stack elements: 30 20 10

Top element: 30

Popped element: 30

Popped element: 20

Stack elements: 10

This demonstrates the basic operations of a stack using linked lists in C.

5.3. Evaluate a post fix expression using a stack

Evaluating a postfix expression involves using a stack to keep track of operands and perform operations based on operators encountered in the expression. Below is a C program that evaluates a postfix expression using a stack:

```c
#include <stdio.h>
#include <stdlib.h>
#include <ctype.h>
// Structure to represent a node in the stack
struct Node
{
   int data;
   struct Node* next;
};
// Structure to represent a stack
struct Stack
{
   struct Node* top;
};
// Function to initialize a stack
struct Stack* createStack()
{
   struct Stack* stack = (struct Stack*)malloc(sizeof(struct Stack));
   stack->top = NULL;
   return stack;
}
// Function to check if the stack is empty
int isEmpty(struct Stack* stack)
{
   return stack->top == NULL;
}
```

```c
// Function to create a new node with the given data
struct Node* createNode(int data)
{
    struct Node* newNode = (struct Node*)malloc(sizeof(struct Node));
    newNode->data = data;
    newNode->next = NULL;
    return newNode;
}
// Function to push an element onto the stack
void push(struct Stack* stack, int item)
{
    struct Node* newNode = createNode(item);
    newNode->next = stack->top;
    stack->top = newNode;
}
// Function to pop an element from the stack
int pop(struct Stack* stack)
{
    if (isEmpty(stack))
    {
        printf("Stack underflow: Cannot pop from an empty stack.\n");
        return -1; // Return an invalid value
    }
    struct Node* poppedNode = stack->top;
    int poppedData = poppedNode->data;
    stack->top = poppedNode->next;
    free(poppedNode);
    return poppedData;
}
```

```c
// Function to evaluate a postfix expression
int evaluatePostfix(char* expression)
{
    struct Stack* stack = createStack();
    for (int i = 0; expression[i] != '\0'; i++)
    {
        if (isdigit(expression[i]))
        {
            // If the character is a digit, push it onto the stack
            push(stack, expression[i] - '0');
        }
        else
        {
            // If the character is an operator, pop two operands, perform the operation, and push the result
            int operand2 = pop(stack);
            int operand1 = pop(stack);
            switch (expression[i])
            {
                case '+':
                    push(stack, operand1 + operand2);
                    break;
                case '-':
                    push(stack, operand1 - operand2);
                    break;
                case '*':
                    push(stack, operand1 * operand2);
                    break;
                case '/':
                    if (operand2 != 0)
                    {
```

```c
                push(stack, operand1 / operand2);
            }
else
{
                printf("Error: Division by zero.\n");
                free(stack);
                return -1; // Return an invalid value
            }
            break;
        default:
            printf("Error: Invalid operator.\n");
            free(stack);
            return -1; // Return an invalid value
        }
    }
  }
  if (!isEmpty(stack))
{
    int result = pop(stack);
    // If the stack is not empty, there might be an issue with the expression
    if (isEmpty(stack))
{
      free(stack);
      return result;
    }
else
{
      printf("Error: Invalid postfix expression.\n");
      free(stack);
      return -1; // Return an invalid value
```

```c
        }
    }
else
{
        printf("Error: Empty postfix expression.\n");
        free(stack);
        return -1; // Return an invalid value
    }
}
int main()
{
    char expression[] = "23*5+";
    // Evaluate the postfix expression
    int result = evaluatePostfix(expression);
    if (result != -1)
{
        printf("Result of postfix expression \"%s\": %d\n", expression, result);
    }
    return 0;
}
```

In this example:

- The Node structure represents a node in the stack.
- The Stack structure represents a stack using a linked list.
- The createStack, isEmpty, createNode, push, and pop functions are used for stack operations.
- The evaluatePostfix function evaluates the postfix expression by scanning each character in the expression, pushing operands onto the stack and performing operations when operators are encountered.

Output

When you run this program with the provided postfix expression "23*5+", it will output:

Result of postfix expression "23*5+": 11

This demonstrates the basic steps of evaluating a postfix expression using a stack in C.

5.4. Use a stack to check for balanced parentheses in an expression

Checking for balanced parentheses in an expression is a common problem that can be efficiently solved using a stack. Below is a C program that uses a stack to check for balanced parentheses in an expression:

```c
#include <stdio.h>
#include <stdlib.h>
// Structure to represent a node in the stack
struct Node
{
    char data;
    struct Node* next;
};
// Structure to represent a stack
struct Stack
{
    struct Node* top;
};
// Function to initialize a stack
struct Stack* createStack()
{
    struct Stack* stack = (struct Stack*)malloc(sizeof(struct Stack));
    stack->top = NULL;
    return stack;
}
// Function to check if the stack is empty
int isEmpty(struct Stack* stack)
{
    return stack->top == NULL;
}
// Function to create a new node with the given data
```

```c
struct Node* createNode(char data)
{
    struct Node* newNode = (struct Node*)malloc(sizeof(struct Node));
    newNode->data = data;
    newNode->next = NULL;
    return newNode;
}
// Function to push a character onto the stack
void push(struct Stack* stack, char item)
{
    struct Node* newNode = createNode(item);
    newNode->next = stack->top;
    stack->top = newNode;
}
// Function to pop a character from the stack
char pop(struct Stack* stack)
{
    if (isEmpty(stack))
    {
        printf("Stack underflow: Cannot pop from an empty stack.\n");
        return '\0'; // Return a null character
    }
    struct Node* poppedNode = stack->top;
    char poppedData = poppedNode->data;
    stack->top = poppedNode->next;
    free(poppedNode);
    return poppedData;
}
// Function to check for balanced parentheses in an expression
int areParenthesesBalanced(char* expression)
```

```c
{
    struct Stack* stack = createStack();
    for (int i = 0; expression[i] != '\0'; i++)
    {
        char currentChar = expression[i];
        if (currentChar == '(' || currentChar == '[' || currentChar == '{')
        {
            // If the character is an opening parenthesis, push it onto the stack
            push(stack, currentChar);
        }
else if (currentChar == ')' || currentChar == ']' || currentChar == '}')
        {
            // If the character is a closing parenthesis, pop from the stack and check for matching pair
            if (isEmpty(stack))
            {
                // If the stack is empty, there is no matching opening parenthesis
                free(stack);
                return 0; // Not balanced
            }
            char poppedChar = pop(stack);
            if ((currentChar == ')' && poppedChar != '(') ||
                (currentChar == ']' && poppedChar != '[') ||
                (currentChar == '}' && poppedChar != '{')) {
                // If the popped character does not match the corresponding opening parenthesis
                free(stack);
                return 0; // Not balanced
            }
        }
    }
```

```c
// After processing the entire expression, the stack should be empty if parentheses are balanced
int result = isEmpty(stack);
// Free the memory allocated for the stack
free(stack);
return result;
}
int main()
{
    char expression1[] = "{[()]}";
    char expression2[] = "([)]";
    // Check for balanced parentheses in the expressions
    int result1 = areParenthesesBalanced(expression1);
    int result2 = areParenthesesBalanced(expression2);
    printf("Expression \"%s\" is %sbalanced.\n", expression1, result1 ? "" : "not ");
    printf("Expression \"%s\" is %sbalanced.\n", expression2, result2 ? "" : "not ");
    return 0;
}
```

In this example:

- The Node structure represents a node in the stack.
- The Stack structure represents a stack using a linked list.
- The createStack, isEmpty, createNode, push, and pop functions are used for stack operations.
- The areParenthesesBalanced function checks for balanced parentheses in an expression by scanning each character in the expression, pushing opening parentheses onto the stack, and popping and checking for matching pairs when closing parentheses are encountered.

Output

When you run this program, it will output:

Expression "{[()]}" is balanced.

Expression "([)]" is not balanced.

This demonstrates the basic steps of using a stack to check for balanced parentheses in C.

6.QUEUE

6.1. Implement a queue using arrays (enqueue and dequeue operations)

Below is a simple implementation of a queue using arrays in C, with enqueue and dequeue operations:

```c
#include <stdio.h>
#include <stdlib.h>
#define MAX_SIZE 100
// Structure to represent a queue
struct Queue
{
    int front, rear, size;
    int array[MAX_SIZE];
};
// Function to initialize a queue
struct Queue* createQueue()
{
    struct Queue* queue = (struct Queue*)malloc(sizeof(struct Queue));
    queue->front = -1;
    queue->rear = -1;
    queue->size = 0;
    return queue;
}
// Function to check if the queue is empty
int isEmpty(struct Queue* queue)
{
    return queue->size == 0;
}
// Function to check if the queue is full
int isFull(struct Queue* queue)
{
```

```c
    return queue->size == MAX_SIZE;
}
// Function to add an element to the rear of the queue (enqueue)
void enqueue(struct Queue* queue, int item)
{
    if (isFull(queue))
    {
        printf("Queue overflow: Cannot enqueue %d, queue is full.\n", item);
        return;
    }
    if (isEmpty(queue))
    {
        // If the queue is empty, set front and rear to 0
        queue->front = 0;
        queue->rear = 0;
    }
else
    {
        // Increment rear circularly
        queue->rear = (queue->rear + 1) % MAX_SIZE;
    }
    queue->array[queue->rear] = item;
    queue->size++;
    printf("%d enqueued to the queue.\n", item);
}
// Function to remove an element from the front of the queue (dequeue)
int dequeue(struct Queue* queue)
{
    if (isEmpty(queue))
    {
```

```c
        printf("Queue underflow: Cannot dequeue from an empty queue.\n");
        return -1; // Return an invalid value
    }
    int dequeuedItem = queue->array[queue->front];
    if (queue->front == queue->rear)
{

        // If there was only one element in the queue, set front and rear to -1
        queue->front = -1;
        queue->rear = -1;

    }
else
{

        // Increment front circularly
        queue->front = (queue->front + 1) % MAX_SIZE;

    }
    queue->size--;
    printf("%d dequeued from the queue.\n", dequeuedItem);
    return dequeuedItem;

}
// Function to get the front element of the queue without dequeuing
int front(struct Queue* queue)
{
    if (isEmpty(queue))
{

        printf("Queue is empty.\n");
        return -1; // Return an invalid value

    }
    return queue->array[queue->front];

}
// Function to print the elements of the queue
```

```c
void printQueue(struct Queue* queue)
{
  if (isEmpty(queue))
{
    printf("Queue is empty.\n");
    return;
  }
  printf("Queue elements: ");
  int i = queue->front;
  do
{
    printf("%d ", queue->array[i]);
    i = (i + 1) % MAX_SIZE;
  }
while (i != (queue->rear + 1) % MAX_SIZE);
  printf("\n");
}
int main()
{
  // Create a queue
  struct Queue* queue = createQueue();
  // Enqueue elements to the queue
  enqueue(queue, 10);
  enqueue(queue, 20);
  enqueue(queue, 30);
  // Print the queue
  printQueue(queue);
  // Get and print the front element without dequeuing
  printf("Front element: %d\n", front(queue));
  // Dequeue elements from the queue
```

```
    dequeue(queue);
    dequeue(queue);
    // Print the updated queue
    printQueue(queue);
    return 0;
}
```

In this example:

- The Queue structure represents a queue with an array.
- The createQueue, isEmpty, isFull, enqueue, dequeue, front, printQueue functions are used for queue operations.
- The main function demonstrates creating a queue, enqueuing elements onto the queue, dequeuing elements from the queue, getting the front element without dequeuing, and printing the queue.

Output

When you run this program, it will output:

```
10 enqueued to the queue.
20 enqueued to the queue.
30 enqueued to the queue.
Queue elements: 10 20 30
Front element: 10
10 dequeued from the queue.
20 dequeued from the queue.
Queue is empty.
```

This demonstrates the basic operations of a queue using arrays in C.

6.2. Implement a queue using linked lists (enqueue and dequeue operations)

Below is a simple implementation of a queue using linked lists in C, with enqueue and dequeue operations:

```c
#include <stdio.h>
#include <stdlib.h>
// Structure to represent a node in the queue
struct Node
{
    int data;
    struct Node* next;
};
// Structure to represent a queue
struct Queue
{
    struct Node* front;
    struct Node* rear;
};
// Function to initialize a queue
struct Queue* createQueue()
{
    struct Queue* queue = (struct Queue*)malloc(sizeof(struct Queue));
    queue->front = NULL;
    queue->rear = NULL;
    return queue;
}
// Function to check if the queue is empty
int isEmpty(struct Queue* queue)
{
    return queue->front == NULL;
}
```

```c
// Function to create a new node with the given data
struct Node* createNode(int data)
{
    struct Node* newNode = (struct Node*)malloc(sizeof(struct Node));
    newNode->data = data;
    newNode->next = NULL;
    return newNode;
}
// Function to add an element to the rear of the queue (enqueue)
void enqueue(struct Queue* queue, int item)
{
    struct Node* newNode = createNode(item);
    if (isEmpty(queue))
    {
        // If the queue is empty, set both front and rear to the new node
        queue->front = newNode;
        queue->rear = newNode;
    }
else
    {
        // Add the new node to the rear
        queue->rear->next = newNode;
        queue->rear = newNode;
    }
    printf("%d enqueued to the queue.\n", item);
}
// Function to remove an element from the front of the queue (dequeue)
int dequeue(struct Queue* queue)
{
    if (isEmpty(queue))
```

```c
{
    printf("Queue underflow: Cannot dequeue from an empty queue.\n");
    return -1; // Return an invalid value
  }
  struct Node* dequeuedNode = queue->front;
  int dequeuedData = dequeuedNode->data;
  if (queue->front == queue->rear)
{
    // If there was only one element in the queue, set both front and rear to NULL
    queue->front = NULL;
    queue->rear = NULL;
  }
else
{
    // Remove the front node
    queue->front = dequeuedNode->next;
  }
  free(dequeuedNode);
  printf("%d dequeued from the queue.\n", dequeuedData);
  return dequeuedData;
}
// Function to get the front element of the queue without dequeuing
int front(struct Queue* queue)
{
  if (isEmpty(queue))
{
    printf("Queue is empty.\n");
    return -1; // Return an invalid value
  }
  return queue->front->data;
```

```c
}
// Function to print the elements of the queue
void printQueue(struct Queue* queue)
{
    if (isEmpty(queue))
    {
        printf("Queue is empty.\n");
        return;
    }
    printf("Queue elements: ");
    struct Node* current = queue->front;
    while (current != NULL)
    {
        printf("%d ", current->data);
        current = current->next;
    }
    printf("\n");
}
// Function to free the memory allocated for the queue
void freeQueue(struct Queue* queue)
{
    while (!isEmpty(queue))
    {
        dequeue(queue);
    }
    free(queue);
}
int main()
{
    // Create a queue
```

```c
    struct Queue* queue = createQueue();
    // Enqueue elements to the queue
    enqueue(queue, 10);
    enqueue(queue, 20);
    enqueue(queue, 30);
    // Print the queue
    printQueue(queue);
    // Get and print the front element without dequeuing
    printf("Front element: %d\n", front(queue));
    // Dequeue elements from the queue
    dequeue(queue);
    dequeue(queue);
    // Print the updated queue
    printQueue(queue);
    // Free the memory allocated for the queue
    freeQueue(queue);
    return 0;
}
```

In this example:

- The Node structure represents a node in the queue.
- The Queue structure represents a queue using a linked list.
- The createQueue, isEmpty, createNode, enqueue, dequeue, front, printQueue, and freeQueue functions are used for queue operations.
- The main function demonstrates creating a queue, enqueuing elements onto the queue, dequeuing elements from the queue, getting the front element without dequeuing, and printing the queue.

Output

When you run this program, it will output:

```
10 enqueued to the queue.
20 enqueued to the queue.
```

30 enqueued to the queue.

Queue elements: 10 20 30

Front element: 10

10 dequeued from the queue.

20 dequeued from the queue.

Queue is empty.

This demonstrates the basic operations of a queue using linked lists in C.

6.3. Circular queue implementation (enqueue and dequeue operations)

Below is a simple implementation of a circular queue using arrays in C, with enqueue and dequeue operations:

```c
#include <stdio.h>
#include <stdlib.h>
#define MAX_SIZE 5
// Structure to represent a circular queue
struct CircularQueue
{
    int front, rear;
    int array[MAX_SIZE];
};
// Function to initialize a circular queue
struct CircularQueue* createCircularQueue()
{
    struct CircularQueue* circularQueue = (struct CircularQueue*)malloc(sizeof(struct
    CircularQueue));
    circularQueue->front = -1;
    circularQueue->rear = -1;
    return circularQueue;
}
// Function to check if the circular queue is empty
int isEmpty(struct CircularQueue* circularQueue)
{
    return circularQueue->front == -1;
}
// Function to check if the circular queue is full
int isFull(struct CircularQueue* circularQueue)
{
    return (circularQueue->rear + 1) % MAX_SIZE == circularQueue->front;
```

```c
}
// Function to add an element to the rear of the circular queue (enqueue)
void enqueue(struct CircularQueue* circularQueue, int item)
{
    if (isFull(circularQueue))
    {
        printf("Circular Queue overflow: Cannot enqueue %d, queue is full.\n", item);
        return;
    }
    if (isEmpty(circularQueue))
    {
        // If the circular queue is empty, set both front and rear to 0
        circularQueue->front = 0;
        circularQueue->rear = 0;
    }
    else
    {
        // Increment rear circularly
        circularQueue->rear = (circularQueue->rear + 1) % MAX_SIZE;
    }
    circularQueue->array[circularQueue->rear] = item;
    printf("%d enqueued to the circular queue.\n", item);
}
// Function to remove an element from the front of the circular queue (dequeue)
int dequeue(struct CircularQueue* circularQueue)
{
    if (isEmpty(circularQueue))
    {
        printf("Circular Queue underflow: Cannot dequeue from an empty queue.\n");
        return -1; // Return an invalid value
```

```c
    }
    int dequeuedItem = circularQueue->array[circularQueue->front];
    if (circularQueue->front == circularQueue->rear)
{
    // If there was only one element in the circular queue, set both front and rear to -1
    circularQueue->front = -1;
    circularQueue->rear = -1;
    }
else
{
    // Increment front circularly
    circularQueue->front = (circularQueue->front + 1) % MAX_SIZE;
    }
    printf("%d dequeued from the circular queue.\n", dequeuedItem);
    return dequeuedItem;
}
// Function to get the front element of the circular queue without dequeuing
int front(struct CircularQueue* circularQueue)
{
    if (isEmpty(circularQueue))
{
    printf("Circular Queue is empty.\n");
    return -1; // Return an invalid value
    }
    return circularQueue->array[circularQueue->front];
}
// Function to print the elements of the circular queue
void printCircularQueue(struct CircularQueue* circularQueue)
{
    if (isEmpty(circularQueue))
```

```c
{
    printf("Circular Queue is empty.\n");
    return;
}
printf("Circular Queue elements: ");
int i = circularQueue->front;
do
{
    printf("%d ", circularQueue->array[i]);
    i = (i + 1) % MAX_SIZE;
}
while (i != (circularQueue->rear + 1) % MAX_SIZE);
printf("\n");
}
int main()
{
    // Create a circular queue
    struct CircularQueue* circularQueue = createCircularQueue();
    // Enqueue elements to the circular queue
    enqueue(circularQueue, 10);
    enqueue(circularQueue, 20);
    enqueue(circularQueue, 30);
    enqueue(circularQueue, 40);
    // Print the circular queue
    printCircularQueue(circularQueue);
    // Get and print the front element without dequeuing
    printf("Front element: %d\n", front(circularQueue));
    // Dequeue elements from the circular queue
    dequeue(circularQueue);
    dequeue(circularQueue);
```

```
// Print the updated circular queue
printCircularQueue(circularQueue);
// Enqueue more elements to the circular queue
enqueue(circularQueue, 50);
enqueue(circularQueue, 60);
// Print the final circular queue
printCircularQueue(circularQueue);
return 0;
}
```

In this example:

- The CircularQueue structure represents a circular queue with an array.
- The createCircularQueue, isEmpty, isFull, enqueue, dequeue, front, printCircularQueue functions are used for circular queue operations.
- The main function demonstrates creating a circular queue, enqueuing elements onto the circular queue, dequeuing elements from the circular queue, getting the front element without dequeuing, and printing the circular queue.

Output

When you run this program, it will output:

```
10 enqueued to the circular queue.
20 enqueued to the circular queue.
30 enqueued to the circular queue.
40 enqueued to the circular queue.
Circular Queue elements: 10 20 30 40
Front element: 10
10 dequeued from the circular queue.
20 dequeued from the circular queue.
Circular Queue elements: 30 40
30 enqueued to the circular queue.
40 enqueued to the circular queue.
```

50 enqueued to the circular queue.

60 enqueued to the circular queue.

Circular Queue elements: 30 40 50 60

This demonstrates the basic operations of a circular queue using arrays in C.

6.4. Simulate a real-world scenario using a queue (Ex. Print queue)

let's simulate a print queue as a real-world scenario using a queue in C programming. In this example, we'll represent print jobs as elements in the queue, and the printing process as dequeueing elements from the queue.

```c
#include <stdio.h>
#include <stdlib.h>
// Structure to represent a node in the queue
struct Node
{
    int jobId;
    struct Node* next;
};
// Structure to represent a print queue
struct PrintQueue
{
    struct Node* front;
    struct Node* rear;
};
// Function to initialize a print queue
struct PrintQueue* createPrintQueue()
{
    struct PrintQueue* printQueue = (struct PrintQueue*)malloc(sizeof(struct PrintQueue));
    printQueue->front = NULL;
    printQueue->rear = NULL;
    return printQueue;
}
// Function to check if the print queue is empty
int isPrintQueueEmpty(struct PrintQueue* printQueue)
{
    return printQueue->front == NULL;
```

```c
}
// Function to create a new print job with the given job ID
struct Node* createPrintJob(int jobId)
{
    struct Node* newPrintJob = (struct Node*)malloc(sizeof(struct Node));
    newPrintJob->jobId = jobId;
    newPrintJob->next = NULL;
    return newPrintJob;
}
// Function to add a print job to the rear of the print queue (enqueue)
void enqueuePrintJob(struct PrintQueue* printQueue, int jobId)
{
    struct Node* newPrintJob = createPrintJob(jobId);
    if (isPrintQueueEmpty(printQueue))
    {
        // If the print queue is empty, set both front and rear to the new print job
        printQueue->front = newPrintJob;
        printQueue->rear = newPrintJob;
    }
else
    {
        // Add the new print job to the rear
        printQueue->rear->next = newPrintJob;
        printQueue->rear = newPrintJob;
    }
    printf("Print Job #%d added to the print queue.\n", jobId);
}
// Function to remove a print job from the front of the print queue (dequeue)
void dequeuePrintJob(struct PrintQueue* printQueue)
{
```

```c
  if (isPrintQueueEmpty(printQueue))
{
    printf("Print Queue is empty. No print jobs to dequeue.\n");
    return;
  }
  struct Node* dequeuedPrintJob = printQueue->front;
  int dequeuedJobId = dequeuedPrintJob->jobId;
  if (printQueue->front == printQueue->rear)
{
    // If there was only one print job in the queue, set both front and rear to NULL
    printQueue->front = NULL;
    printQueue->rear = NULL;
  }
else
{
    // Remove the front print job
    printQueue->front = dequeuedPrintJob->next;
  }
  free(dequeuedPrintJob);
  printf("Print Job #%d dequeued and sent to the printer.\n", dequeuedJobId);
}
// Function to print the current print queue
void printPrintQueue(struct PrintQueue* printQueue)
{
  if (isPrintQueueEmpty(printQueue))
{
    printf("Print Queue is empty.\n");
    return;
  }
```

```c
    printf("Print Queue (Job IDs): ");
    struct Node* current = printQueue->front;
    while (current != NULL)
{

    printf("%d ", current->jobId);
    current = current->next;
}
    printf("\n");
}
// Function to free the memory allocated for the print queue
void freePrintQueue(struct PrintQueue* printQueue)
{
    while (!isPrintQueueEmpty(printQueue))
{

    dequeuePrintJob(printQueue);
}
    free(printQueue);
}
int main()
{
    // Create a print queue
    struct PrintQueue* printQueue = createPrintQueue();
    // Enqueue print jobs
    enqueuePrintJob(printQueue, 101);
    enqueuePrintJob(printQueue, 102);
    enqueuePrintJob(printQueue, 103);
    // Print the current print queue
    printPrintQueue(printQueue);
    // Dequeue print jobs (simulate printing process)
    dequeuePrintJob(printQueue);
```

```
dequeuePrintJob(printQueue);
// Print the updated print queue
printPrintQueue(printQueue);
// Enqueue more print jobs
enqueuePrintJob(printQueue, 104);
enqueuePrintJob(printQueue, 105);
// Print the final print queue
printPrintQueue(printQueue);
// Free the memory allocated for the print queue
freePrintQueue(printQueue);
return 0;
}
```

In this example:

- The PrintQueue structure represents a print queue using a linked list.
- The createPrintQueue, isPrintQueueEmpty, createPrintJob, enqueuePrintJob, dequeuePrintJob, printPrintQueue, and freePrintQueue functions are used for print queue operations.
- The main function demonstrates creating a print queue, enqueuing print jobs, dequeuing print jobs (simulating the printing process), printing the print queue, and freeing the memory allocated for the print queue.

Output

When you run this program, it will output:

```
Print Job #101 added to the print queue.
Print Job #102 added to the print queue.
Print Job #103 added to the print queue.
Print Queue (Job IDs): 101 102 103
Print Job #101 dequeued and sent to the printer.
Print Job #102 dequeued and sent to the printer.
Print Queue (Job IDs): 103
Print Job #103 dequeued and sent to the printer.
```

Print Queue is empty. No print jobs to dequeue.

Print Job #104 added to the print queue.

Print Job #105 added to the print queue.

Print Queue (Job IDs): 104 105

Print Job #104 dequeued and sent to the printer.

Print Job #105 dequeued and sent to the printer.

Print Queue is empty. No print jobs to dequeue.

This simulates a simple print queue scenario using a linked list-based queue in C.

7. TREE

7.1. Binary tree traversal
7.1.1. In-order

Consider a binary tree node structure:

```c
#include <stdio.h>
#include <stdlib.h>
struct Node
{
    int data;
    struct Node* left;
    struct Node* right;
};
// Function to create a new node
struct Node* createNode(int data)
{
    struct Node* newNode = (struct Node*)malloc(sizeof(struct Node));
    if (newNode == NULL)
    {
        printf("Memory allocation failed.\n");
        exit(EXIT_FAILURE);
    }
    newNode->data = data;
    newNode->left = NULL;
    newNode->right = NULL;
    return newNode;
}
// Function for in-order traversal of a binary tree
void inOrderTraversal(struct Node* root)
{
    if (root != NULL)
    {
```

```c
        inOrderTraversal(root->left);
        printf("%d ", root->data);
        inOrderTraversal(root->right);
    }
}
int main()
{
    // Create a sample binary tree
    struct Node* root = createNode(1);
    root->left = createNode(2);
    root->right = createNode(3);
    root->left->left = createNode(4);
    root->left->right = createNode(5);
    // Perform in-order traversal
    printf("In-order traversal: ");
    inOrderTraversal(root);
    printf("\n");
    return 0;
}
```

In this example, the inOrderTraversal function recursively traverses the binary tree in in-order fashion: left subtree, current node, right subtree. The main function creates a simple binary tree and calls the in-order traversal function.

Output

When you run this program, it will output:

In-order traversal: 4 2 5 1 3

This represents the in-order traversal of the binary tree. Adjust the tree structure based on your specific use case or data.

7.1.2. Pre-order

Here's an example of how you might implement pre-order traversal of a binary tree in C:

```c
#include <stdio.h>
#include <stdlib.h>
struct Node
{
   int data;
   struct Node* left;
   struct Node* right;
};
// Function to create a new node
struct Node* createNode(int data)
{
   struct Node* newNode = (struct Node*)malloc(sizeof(struct Node));
   if (newNode == NULL)
{

     printf("Memory allocation failed.\n");
     exit(EXIT_FAILURE);

   }
   newNode->data = data;
   newNode->left = NULL;
   newNode->right = NULL;
   return newNode;
}
// Function for pre-order traversal of a binary tree
void preOrderTraversal(struct Node* root)
{
   if (root != NULL)
{

     printf("%d ", root->data);
```

```c
        preOrderTraversal(root->left);

        preOrderTraversal(root->right);

    }

}

int main()

{

    // Create a sample binary tree

    struct Node* root = createNode(1);

    root->left = createNode(2);

    root->right = createNode(3);

    root->left->left = createNode(4);

    root->left->right = createNode(5);

    // Perform pre-order traversal

    printf("Pre-order traversal: ");

    preOrderTraversal(root);

    printf("\n");

    return 0;

}
```

In this example, the preOrderTraversal function recursively traverses the binary tree in pre-order fashion: current node, left subtree, right subtree. The main function creates a simple binary tree and calls the pre-order traversal function.

Output

When you run this program, it will output:

Pre-order traversal: 1 2 4 5 3

This represents the pre-order traversal of the binary tree. Adjust the tree structure based on your specific use case or data.

7.1.3.Post-order

Below is an example of how you might implement post-order traversal of a binary tree in C:

```c
#include <stdio.h>
#include <stdlib.h>
struct Node
{
   int data;
   struct Node* left;
   struct Node* right;
};
// Function to create a new node
struct Node* createNode(int data)
{
   struct Node* newNode = (struct Node*)malloc(sizeof(struct Node));
   if (newNode == NULL)
   {
      printf("Memory allocation failed.\n");
      exit(EXIT_FAILURE);
   }
   newNode->data = data;
   newNode->left = NULL;
   newNode->right = NULL;
   return newNode;
}
// Function for post-order traversal of a binary tree
void postOrderTraversal(struct Node* root)
{
   if (root != NULL)
   {
```

```c
    postOrderTraversal(root->left);
    postOrderTraversal(root->right);
    printf("%d ", root->data);
  }
}
int main()
{
  // Create a sample binary tree
  struct Node* root = createNode(1);
  root->left = createNode(2);
  root->right = createNode(3);
  root->left->left = createNode(4);
  root->left->right = createNode(5);
  // Perform post-order traversal
  printf("Post-order traversal: ");
  postOrderTraversal(root);
  printf("\n");
  return 0;
}
```

In this example, the postOrderTraversal function recursively traverses the binary tree in post-order fashion: left subtree, right subtree, current node. The main function creates a simple binary tree and calls the post-order traversal function.

Output

When you run this program, it will output:

Post-order traversal: 4 5 2 3 1

This represents the post-order traversal of the binary tree. Adjust the tree structure based on your specific use case or data.

7.2. Find the height of a binary tree.

To find the height of a binary tree in C programming, you can implement a recursive function that traverses the tree and calculates the height. The height of a binary tree is the length of the longest path from the root node to a leaf node.

Here's an example:

```c
#include <stdio.h>
#include <stdlib.h>
struct Node
{
    int data;
    struct Node* left;
    struct Node* right;
};
// Function to create a new node
struct Node* createNode(int data)
{
    struct Node* newNode = (struct Node*)malloc(sizeof(struct Node));
    if (newNode == NULL) {
        printf("Memory allocation failed.\n");
        exit(EXIT_FAILURE);
    }
    newNode->data = data;
    newNode->left = NULL;
    newNode->right = NULL;
    return newNode;
}
// Function to find the height of a binary tree
int findHeight(struct Node* root)
{
    if (root == NULL)
```

```c
{
    return -1; // Height of an empty tree is -1
}
else
{
    int leftHeight = findHeight(root->left);
    int rightHeight = findHeight(root->right);
    // Return the maximum height of the left and right subtrees, plus 1 for the current node
    return (leftHeight > rightHeight) ? leftHeight + 1 : rightHeight + 1;
  }
}
int main()
{
  // Create a sample binary tree
  struct Node* root = createNode(1);
  root->left = createNode(2);
  root->right = createNode(3);
  root->left->left = createNode(4);
  root->left->right = createNode(5);
  // Find the height of the binary tree
  int height = findHeight(root);
  // Print the height
  printf("Height of the binary tree: %d\n", height);
  return 0;
}
```

In this example, the findHeight function is a recursive function that calculates the height of the binary tree. It returns -1 for an empty tree and calculates the height as the maximum of the heights of the left and right subtrees plus 1 for the current node.

Output

When you run this program, it will output:

Height of the binary tree: 2

Adjust the tree structure based on your specific use case or data.

7.3. Binary Search tree insert operation

To perform the insert operation in a Binary Search Tree (BST) in C programming, you need to create a function that recursively inserts a new node while maintaining the properties of the BST. The BST property ensures that for each node, all nodes in its left subtree have values less than the node, and all nodes in its right subtree have values greater than the node. Here's an example implementation:

```c
#include <stdio.h>
#include <stdlib.h>
// Structure for a node in the Binary Search Tree
struct Node
{
    int data;
    struct Node* left;
    struct Node* right;
};
// Function to create a new node with the given data
struct Node* createNode(int data)
{
    struct Node* newNode = (struct Node*)malloc(sizeof(struct Node));
    if (newNode == NULL)
    {
        printf("Memory allocation failed.\n");
        exit(EXIT_FAILURE);
    }
    newNode->data = data;
    newNode->left = NULL;
    newNode->right = NULL;
    return newNode;
}
// Function to insert a new node into the Binary Search Tree
```

```c
struct Node* insert(struct Node* root, int data)
{
    // If the tree is empty, create a new node
    if (root == NULL) {
        return createNode(data);
    }
    // Otherwise, recursively insert into the left or right subtree
    if (data < root->data)
{
        root->left = insert(root->left, data);
    }
else if (data > root->data)
{
        root->right = insert(root->right, data);
    }
    // Return the updated root
    return root;
}
// Function to perform in-order traversal of the Binary Search Tree
void inOrderTraversal(struct Node* root)
{
    if (root != NULL)
{
        inOrderTraversal(root->left);
        printf("%d ", root->data);
        inOrderTraversal(root->right);
    }
}
int main()
{
```

```c
// Create an empty Binary Search Tree
struct Node* root = NULL;
// Insert nodes into the Binary Search Tree
root = insert(root, 50);
insert(root, 30);
insert(root, 20);
insert(root, 40);
insert(root, 70);
insert(root, 60);
insert(root, 80);
// Perform in-order traversal to display the sorted values
printf("In-order traversal: ");
inOrderTraversal(root);
printf("\n");
return 0;
}
```

In this example, the insert function recursively inserts a new node into the BST. The inOrderTraversal function is used to perform an in-order traversal to display the sorted values of the BST.

Output

When you run this program, it will output:

In-order traversal: 20 30 40 50 60 70 80

This represents the values of the nodes in ascending order, demonstrating that the BST property is maintained. Adjust the values and structure of the tree based on your specific use case or data.

7.4. Binary Search tree delete operation

The delete operation in a Binary Search Tree (BST) is more complex than the insert operation because it involves handling different cases. There are three main cases to consider when deleting a node from a BST:

- Node with No Children (Leaf Node): Simply remove the node.
- Node with One Child: Replace the node with its child.
- Node with Two Children: Find the node's in-order successor (or predecessor), copy its data to the node to be deleted, and then recursively delete the in-order successor (which is in the left subtree for the successor, or in the right subtree for the predecessor).

Here's an example implementation of the delete operation in a BST in C:

```c
#include <stdio.h>
#include <stdlib.h>
// Structure for a node in the Binary Search Tree
struct Node
{
   int data;
   struct Node* left;
   struct Node* right;
};
// Function to create a new node with the given data
struct Node* createNode(int data)
{
   struct Node* newNode = (struct Node*)malloc(sizeof(struct Node));
   if (newNode == NULL)
{
      printf("Memory allocation failed.\n");
      exit(EXIT_FAILURE);
   }
   newNode->data = data;
   newNode->left = NULL;
```

```c
    newNode->right = NULL;
    return newNode;
}
// Function to find the in-order successor
struct Node* findInOrderSuccessor(struct Node* node)
{
    while (node->left != NULL)
    {
        node = node->left;
    }
    return node;
}
// Function to delete a node with the given data from the Binary Search Tree
struct Node* deleteNode(struct Node* root, int data)
{
    if (root == NULL)
    {
        return root;
    }
    // Traverse the tree to find the node to be deleted
    if (data < root->data)
    {
        root->left = deleteNode(root->left, data);
    }
else if (data > root->data)
    {
        root->right = deleteNode(root->right, data);
    }
else
    {
```

```c
        // Node to be deleted found
        // Case 1: Node with only one child or no child
        if (root->left == NULL)
{
            struct Node* temp = root->right;
            free(root);
            return temp;
        }
else if (root->right == NULL)
{
            struct Node* temp = root->left;
            free(root);
            return temp;
        }
        // Case 3: Node with two children
        struct Node* inOrderSuccessor = findInOrderSuccessor(root->right);
        root->data = inOrderSuccessor->data;
        root->right = deleteNode(root->right, inOrderSuccessor->data);
    }
    return root;
}
// Function to perform in-order traversal of the Binary Search Tree
void inOrderTraversal(struct Node* root)
{
    if (root != NULL)
    {
        inOrderTraversal(root->left);
        printf("%d ", root->data);
        inOrderTraversal(root->right);
    }
```

```c
}
int main()
{
    // Create a Binary Search Tree
    struct Node* root = createNode(50);
    root->left = createNode(30);
    root->right = createNode(70);
    root->left->left = createNode(20);
    root->left->right = createNode(40);
    root->right->left = createNode(60);
    root->right->right = createNode(80);
    // Perform in-order traversal before deletion
    printf("In-order traversal before deletion: ");
    inOrderTraversal(root);
    printf("\n");
    // Delete a node (for example, deleting node with data 30)
    root = deleteNode(root, 30);
    // Perform in-order traversal after deletion
    printf("In-order traversal after deletion: ");
    inOrderTraversal(root);
    printf("\n");
    return 0;
}
```

In this example, the deleteNode function handles the three cases mentioned above. The findInOrderSuccessor function is used to find the in-order successor of a node.

Output

When you run this program, it will output:

In-order traversal before deletion: 20 30 40 50 60 70 80

In-order traversal after deletion: 20 40 50 60 70 80

7.5. Binary Search tree search operation

In a Binary Search Tree (BST), the search operation involves traversing the tree to find a specific value. The key property of a BST is that for each node, all nodes in its left subtree have values less than the node, and all nodes in its right subtree have values greater than the node. This property allows us to efficiently search for a value by comparing it with the values in the nodes during traversal. Here's an example implementation of the search operation in a BST in C:

```c
#include <stdio.h>
#include <stdlib.h>
// Structure for a node in the Binary Search Tree
struct Node
{
   int data;
   struct Node* left;
   struct Node* right;
};
// Function to create a new node with the given data
struct Node* createNode(int data)
{
   struct Node* newNode = (struct Node*)malloc(sizeof(struct Node));
   if (newNode == NULL)
   {
      printf("Memory allocation failed.\n");
      exit(EXIT_FAILURE);
   }
   newNode->data = data;
   newNode->left = NULL;
   newNode->right = NULL;
   return newNode;
}
// Function to search for a value in the Binary Search Tree
```

```c
struct Node* search(struct Node* root, int key)
{
    // If the tree is empty or the key is present at the root
    if (root == NULL || root->data == key)
    {
        return root;
    }
    // If the key is smaller than the root's key, search in the left subtree
    if (key < root->data)
    {
        return search(root->left, key);
    }
    // If the key is larger than the root's key, search in the right subtree
    return search(root->right, key);
}
// Function to perform in-order traversal of the Binary Search Tree
void inOrderTraversal(struct Node* root)
{
    if (root != NULL)
    {
        inOrderTraversal(root->left);
        printf("%d ", root->data);
        inOrderTraversal(root->right);
    }
}
int main()
{
    // Create a Binary Search Tree
    struct Node* root = createNode(50);
    root->left = createNode(30);
```

```c
    root->right = createNode(70);
    root->left->left = createNode(20);
    root->left->right = createNode(40);
    root->right->left = createNode(60);
    root->right->right = createNode(80);
    // Perform in-order traversal
    printf("In-order traversal: ");
    inOrderTraversal(root);
    printf("\n");
    // Search for a value (for example, searching for the value 40)
    int keyToSearch = 40;
    struct Node* result = search(root, keyToSearch);
    // Check if the value is found
    if (result != NULL)
{
        printf("Value %d found in the Binary Search Tree.\n", keyToSearch);
    }
else
{
        printf("Value %d not found in the Binary Search Tree.\n", keyToSearch);
    }
    return 0;
}
```

In this example, the search function recursively searches for a value in the BST. The inOrderTraversal function is used to perform an in-order traversal to display the sorted values of the BST.

Output

When you run this program, it will output:

In-order traversal: 20 30 40 50 60 70 80

Value 40 found in the Binary Search Tree.

7.6.AVL tree (or) Red-black tree implementation

Implementing AVL trees or red-black trees requires a bit more complexity compared to binary search trees due to the need to maintain balance or satisfy certain properties. Below is an example of an AVL tree implementation in C. The AVL tree is a self-balancing binary search tree, where the heights of the two child subtrees of any node differ by at most one.

```c
#include <stdio.h>
#include <stdlib.h>
// Structure for a node in the AVL Tree
struct AVLNode
{
    int data;
    struct AVLNode* left;
    struct AVLNode* right;
    int height;
};
// Function to get the height of a node
int getHeight(struct AVLNode* node)
{
    if (node == NULL)
    {
        return 0;
    }
    return node->height;
}
// Function to update the height of a node based on the heights of its children
void updateHeight(struct AVLNode* node)
{
    if (node != NULL)
    {
        int leftHeight = getHeight(node->left);
```

```c
        int rightHeight = getHeight(node->right);
        node->height = (leftHeight > rightHeight ? leftHeight : rightHeight) + 1;
    }
}
// Function to perform a right rotation on the given node
struct AVLNode* rightRotate(struct AVLNode* y)
{
    struct AVLNode* x = y->left;
    struct AVLNode* T2 = x->right;
    // Perform rotation
    x->right = y;
    y->left = T2;
    // Update heights
    updateHeight(y);
    updateHeight(x);
    // Return new root
    return x;
}
// Function to perform a left rotation on the given node
struct AVLNode* leftRotate(struct AVLNode* x)
{
    struct AVLNode* y = x->right;
    struct AVLNode* T2 = y->left;
    // Perform rotation
    y->left = x;
    x->right = T2;
    // Update heights
    updateHeight(x);
    updateHeight(y);
    // Return new root
```

```c
    return y;
}
// Function to balance the AVL tree after a node is inserted
struct AVLNode* balance(struct AVLNode* root, int data)
{
    // Update height of the current node
    updateHeight(root);
    // Calculate the balance factor
    int balanceFactor = getHeight(root->left) - getHeight(root->right);
    // Left Heavy (LL or LR)
    if (balanceFactor > 1 && data < root->left->data)
    {
        return rightRotate(root);
    }
    // Right Heavy (RR or RL)
    if (balanceFactor < -1 && data > root->right->data)
    {
        return leftRotate(root);
    }
    // Left Right Heavy (LR)
    if (balanceFactor > 1 && data > root->left->data)
    {
        root->left = leftRotate(root->left);
        return rightRotate(root);
    }
    // Right Left Heavy (RL)
    if (balanceFactor < -1 && data < root->right->data)
    {
        root->right = rightRotate(root->right);
        return leftRotate(root);
```

```c
    }
    // No need for balancing
    return root;
}
// Function to insert a new node into the AVL Tree
struct AVLNode* insert(struct AVLNode* root, int data)
{
    // Perform standard BST insertion
    if (root == NULL)
    {
        struct AVLNode* newNode = (struct AVLNode*)malloc(sizeof(struct AVLNode));
        newNode->data = data;
        newNode->left = NULL;
        newNode->right = NULL;
        newNode->height = 1; // New node is at height 1
        return newNode;
    }
    if (data < root->data)
    {
        root->left = insert(root->left, data);
    }
else if (data > root->data)
    {
        root->right = insert(root->right, data);
    }
else
    {
        // Duplicate data not allowed
        return root;
    }
```

```c
    // Update height of the current node
    updateHeight(root);
    // Balance the tree
    return balance(root, data);
}
// Function to perform in-order traversal of the AVL Tree
void inOrderTraversal(struct AVLNode* root)
{
    if (root != NULL)
    {
        inOrderTraversal(root->left);
        printf("%d ", root->data);
        inOrderTraversal(root->right);
    }
}
int main()
{
    struct AVLNode* root = NULL;
    // Insert nodes into the AVL Tree
    root = insert(root, 10);
    root = insert(root, 20);
    root = insert(root, 30);
    root = insert(root, 40);
    root = insert(root, 50);
    root = insert(root, 25);
    // Perform in-order traversal
    printf("In-order traversal: ");
    inOrderTraversal(root);
    printf("\n");
```

```
    return 0;
}
```

In this example, the insert function inserts a new node into the AVL tree and calls the balance function to ensure that the tree remains balanced after insertion.

Keep in mind that AVL trees are just one form of self-balancing binary search trees. Red-Black trees are another popular option. The implementation would be similar in structure but may differ in specific details.

7.7. Check if a binary tree is balanced

To check if a binary tree is balanced, you can write a function that recursively calculates the height of the left and right subtrees for each node and checks if the difference in height is within a specified range (typically 1). A balanced binary tree ensures that the heights of the left and right subtrees of every node differ by at most 1. Here's an example implementation in C:

```c
#include <stdio.h>
#include <stdlib.h>
// Structure for a node in the Binary Tree
struct Node
{
    int data;
    struct Node* left;
    struct Node* right;
};
// Function to create a new node with the given data
struct Node* createNode(int data)
{
    struct Node* newNode = (struct Node*)malloc(sizeof(struct Node));
    if (newNode == NULL)
    {
        printf("Memory allocation failed.\n");
        exit(EXIT_FAILURE);
    }
    newNode->data = data;
    newNode->left = NULL;
    newNode->right = NULL;
    return newNode;
}
// Function to calculate the height of a binary tree
int calculateHeight(struct Node* root)
```

```c
{
  if (root == NULL)
  {
      return 0;
  }
  int leftHeight = calculateHeight(root->left);
  int rightHeight = calculateHeight(root->right);
  // Return the maximum of left and right subtree heights, plus 1 for the current node
  return (leftHeight > rightHeight) ? leftHeight + 1 : rightHeight + 1;
}
// Function to check if a binary tree is balanced
int isBalanced(struct Node* root)
{
  if (root == NULL) {
      return 1; // An empty tree is always balanced
  }
  int leftHeight = calculateHeight(root->left);
  int rightHeight = calculateHeight(root->right);
  // Check if the subtree heights differ by at most 1
  if (abs(leftHeight - rightHeight) <= 1 &&
     isBalanced(root->left) &&
     isBalanced(root->right))
  {
      return 1; // Balanced
  }
  return 0; // Not balanced
}
int main()
{
  // Create an unbalanced binary tree
```

```c
    struct Node* root = createNode(1);
    root->left = createNode(2);
    root->right = createNode(3);
    root->left->left = createNode(4);
    root->left->left->left = createNode(5);
    // Check if the binary tree is balanced
    if (isBalanced(root))
{

    printf("The binary tree is balanced.\n");

}
else
{

    printf("The binary tree is not balanced.\n");

}
    return 0;

}
```

In this example, the calculateHeight function calculates the height of a binary tree, and the isBalanced function checks if the tree is balanced by comparing the heights of the left and right subtrees at each node.

Output

The given binary tree is unbalanced, and the output will be:

The binary tree is not balanced.

Adjust the tree structure based on your specific use case or data.

7.8.Convert a binary search tree to a doubly linked list

To convert a Binary Search Tree (BST) to a doubly linked list (DLL), you can perform an in-order traversal of the tree and modify the tree nodes to form a DLL. During the traversal, you update the left pointers to represent the previous node in the DLL and the right pointers to represent the next node. Here's an example implementation in C:

```c
#include <stdio.h>
#include <stdlib.h>
// Structure for a node in the Binary Search Tree
struct Node
{
   int data;
   struct Node* left;
   struct Node* right;
};
// Function to create a new node with the given data
struct Node* createNode(int data)
{
   struct Node* newNode = (struct Node*)malloc(sizeof(struct Node));
   if (newNode == NULL)
   {
      printf("Memory allocation failed.\n");
      exit(EXIT_FAILURE);
   }
   newNode->data = data;
   newNode->left = NULL;
   newNode->right = NULL;
   return newNode;
}
// Function to perform in-order traversal and convert BST to DLL
void convertToDLL(struct Node* root, struct Node** prev, struct Node** head)
```

```c
{
    if (root == NULL)
    {
        return;
    }
    // Recursively convert left subtree
    convertToDLL(root->left, prev, head);
    // Modify pointers to form the DLL
    if (*prev == NULL)
    {
        // If prev is NULL, it means we are at the leftmost node of the BST
        *head = root;
    }
else
    {
        // Otherwise, update right pointer of the previous node
        (*prev)->right = root;
        // Update left pointer of the current node
        root->left = *prev;
    }
    // Update the previous node to the current node
    *prev = root;
    // Recursively convert right subtree
    convertToDLL(root->right, prev, head);
}
// Function to print the doubly linked list
void printDLL(struct Node* head)
{
    while (head != NULL)
    {
```

```c
        printf("%d ", head->data);
        head = head->right;
    }
    printf("\n");
}
int main()
{
    // Create a Binary Search Tree
    struct Node* root = createNode(4);
    root->left = createNode(2);
    root->right = createNode(5);
    root->left->left = createNode(1);
    root->left->right = createNode(3);
    // Convert BST to DLL
    struct Node* prev = NULL;
    struct Node* head = NULL;
    convertToDLL(root, &prev, &head);
    // Print the doubly linked list
    printf("Doubly Linked List: ");
    printDLL(head);
    return 0;
}
```

In this example, the convertToDLL function performs in-order traversal of the BST and modifies the pointers to form a doubly linked list. The printDLL function is used to print the elements of the doubly linked list.

Output

When you run this program, it will output:

Doubly Linked List: 1 2 3 4 5

This represents the elements of the BST printed in sorted order, confirming that the conversion to a doubly linked list is successful. Adjust the tree structure based on your specific use case or data.

8.GRAPHS

8.1. Implement an adjacency matrix

An adjacency matrix is a square matrix used to represent a finite graph. In the context of graphs, the elements of the matrix indicate whether pairs of vertices are adjacent or not in the graph. The diagonal elements of the matrix are typically used to represent self-loops in the graph. Here's a simple implementation of an adjacency matrix in C:

```c
#include <stdio.h>
#include <stdlib.h>
// Maximum number of vertices in the graph
#define MAX_VERTICES 100
// Structure to represent an adjacency matrix
struct Graph
{
   int vertices;
   int matrix[MAX_VERTICES][MAX_VERTICES];
};
// Function to initialize an empty graph with a given number of vertices
void initializeGraph(struct Graph *graph, int vertices)
{
   if (vertices > MAX_VERTICES)
   {
       printf("Number of vertices exceeds the maximum limit.\n");
       exit(EXIT_FAILURE);
   }
   graph->vertices = vertices;
   // Initialize the matrix with zeros
   for (int i = 0; i < vertices; ++i)
   {
       for (int j = 0; j < vertices; ++j)
       {
```

```c
        graph->matrix[i][j] = 0;
    }
  }
}
// Function to add an edge between two vertices in the graph
void addEdge(struct Graph *graph, int from, int to)
{
  if (from >= 0 && from < graph->vertices && to >= 0 && to < graph->vertices)
  {
      // Assuming an undirected graph, so update both matrix entries
      graph->matrix[from][to] = 1;
      graph->matrix[to][from] = 1;
  }
else
  {
      printf("Invalid vertices.\n");
  }
}
// Function to print the adjacency matrix of the graph
void printGraph(struct Graph *graph)
{
  printf("Adjacency Matrix:\n");
  for (int i = 0; i < graph->vertices; ++i)
  {
      for (int j = 0; j < graph->vertices; ++j)
  {
        printf("%d ", graph->matrix[i][j]);
      }
      printf("\n");
  }
```

```c
}
int main()
{
    // Create a graph with 5 vertices
    struct Graph myGraph;
    initializeGraph(&myGraph, 5);
    // Add edges to the graph
    addEdge(&myGraph, 0, 1);
    addEdge(&myGraph, 0, 4);
    addEdge(&myGraph, 1, 2);
    addEdge(&myGraph, 1, 3);
    addEdge(&myGraph, 1, 4);
    addEdge(&myGraph, 2, 3);
    addEdge(&myGraph, 3, 4);
    // Print the adjacency matrix
    printGraph(&myGraph);
    return 0;
}
```

In this example, the Graph structure represents an adjacency matrix. The initializeGraph function initializes the matrix with zeros, and the addEdge function adds edges by updating the corresponding entries in the matrix.

Output

When you run this program, it will output the adjacency matrix for the given graph:

Adjacency Matrix:

```
0 1 0 0 1
1 0 1 1 1
0 1 0 1 0
0 1 1 0 1
1 1 0 1 0
```

8.2. Implement an adjacency list

An adjacency list is a collection of unordered lists or arrays used to represent a finite graph. Each list corresponds to a vertex in the graph and contains the vertices adjacent to that vertex. Here's a simple implementation of an adjacency list in C:

```c
#include <stdio.h>
#include <stdlib.h>
// Structure to represent a node in the adjacency list
struct Node
{
    int data;
    struct Node* next;
};
// Structure to represent an adjacency list
struct Graph
{
    int vertices;
    struct Node** array;
};
// Function to create a new node with the given data
struct Node* createNode(int data)
{
    struct Node* newNode = (struct Node*)malloc(sizeof(struct Node));
    if (newNode == NULL)
    {
        printf("Memory allocation failed.\n");
        exit(EXIT_FAILURE);
    }
    newNode->data = data;
    ncwNode->next = NULL;
    return newNode;
```

```c
}
// Function to initialize an empty graph with a given number of vertices
struct Graph* initializeGraph(int vertices)
{
    struct Graph* graph = (struct Graph*)malloc(sizeof(struct Graph));
    if (graph == NULL)
    {
        printf("Memory allocation failed.\n");
        exit(EXIT_FAILURE);
    }
    graph->vertices = vertices;
    // Create an array of linked lists (one for each vertex)
    graph->array = (struct Node**)malloc(vertices * sizeof(struct Node*));
    if (graph->array == NULL)
    {
        printf("Memory allocation failed.\n");
        exit(EXIT_FAILURE);
    }
    // Initialize each list as empty
    for (int i = 0; i < vertices; ++i)
    {
        graph->array[i] = NULL;
    }
    return graph;
}
// Function to add an edge between two vertices in the graph
void addEdge(struct Graph* graph, int from, int to)
{
    if (from >= 0 && from < graph->vertices && to >= 0 && to < graph->vertices)
    {
```

```c
    // Create a new node for the 'to' vertex and add it to the list for 'from' vertex
    struct Node* newNode = createNode(to);
    newNode->next = graph->array[from];
    graph->array[from] = newNode;
    // Assuming an undirected graph, add an edge in the other direction as well
    newNode = createNode(from);
    newNode->next = graph->array[to];
    graph->array[to] = newNode;
  }
else
{
    printf("Invalid vertices.\n");
  }
}
// Function to print the adjacency list of the graph
void printGraph(struct Graph* graph)
{
  printf("Adjacency List:\n");
  for (int i = 0; i < graph->vertices; ++i)
{
    printf("%d -> ", i);
    struct Node* current = graph->array[i];
    while (current != NULL)
{
      printf("%d ", current->data);
      current = current->next;
    }
    printf("\n");
  }
}
```

```c
int main()
{
    // Create a graph with 5 vertices
    struct Graph* myGraph = initializeGraph(5);
    // Add edges to the graph
    addEdge(myGraph, 0, 1);
    addEdge(myGraph, 0, 4);
    addEdge(myGraph, 1, 2);
    addEdge(myGraph, 1, 3);
    addEdge(myGraph, 1, 4);
    addEdge(myGraph, 2, 3);
    addEdge(myGraph, 3, 4);
    // Print the adjacency list
    printGraph(myGraph);
    return 0;
}
```

In this example, the Graph structure represents an adjacency list. The initializeGraph function initializes an array of linked lists, where each list corresponds to a vertex in the graph. The addEdge function adds edges by creating nodes for the adjacent vertices and adding them to the corresponding linked lists.

Output

When you run this program, it will output the adjacency list for the given graph:

Adjacency List:

$$0 \rightarrow 4\ 1$$
$$1 \rightarrow 4\ 3\ 2\ 0$$
$$2 \rightarrow 3\ 1$$
$$3 \rightarrow 4\ 2\ 1$$
$$4 \rightarrow 3\ 1\ 0$$

This list indicates the connections between vertices in the graph. Adjust the number of vertices and edges based on your specific use case or data.

8.3.DFS

Depth-First Search (DFS) is an algorithm used to traverse or search through graph or tree structures. It explores as far as possible along each branch before backtracking. Below is an example of implementing Depth-First Search in C for a graph represented using an adjacency list.

```c
#include <stdio.h>
#include <stdlib.h>
// Structure to represent a node in the adjacency list
struct Node
{
   int data;
   struct Node* next;
};
// Structure to represent a graph
struct Graph
{
   int vertices;
   struct Node** array;
};
// Function to create a new node with the given data
struct Node* createNode(int data)
{
   struct Node* newNode = (struct Node*)malloc(sizeof(struct Node));
   if (newNode == NULL)
   {
      printf("Memory allocation failed.\n");
      exit(EXIT_FAILURE);
   }
   newNode->data = data;
   newNode->next = NULL;
```

```c
    return newNode;
}
// Function to initialize a graph with a given number of vertices
struct Graph* initializeGraph(int vertices)
{
    struct Graph* graph = (struct Graph*)malloc(sizeof(struct Graph));
    if (graph == NULL)
    {
        printf("Memory allocation failed.\n");
        exit(EXIT_FAILURE);
    }
    graph->vertices = vertices;
    // Create an array of linked lists (one for each vertex)
    graph->array = (struct Node**)malloc(vertices * sizeof(struct Node*));
    if (graph->array == NULL)
    {
        printf("Memory allocation failed.\n");
        exit(EXIT_FAILURE);
    }
    // Initialize each list as empty
    for (int i = 0; i < vertices; ++i)
    {
        graph->array[i] = NULL;
    }
    return graph;
}
// Function to add an edge between two vertices in the graph
void addEdge(struct Graph* graph, int from, int to)
{
    if (from >= 0 && from < graph->vertices && to >= 0 && to < graph->vertices)
```

```c
{
    // Create a new node for the 'to' vertex and add it to the list for 'from' vertex
    struct Node* newNode = createNode(to);
    newNode->next = graph->array[from];
    graph->array[from] = newNode;
  }
else
{
    printf("Invalid vertices.\n");
  }
}
// Function to perform Depth-First Search
void DFS(struct Graph* graph, int vertex, int* visited)
{
  // Mark the current vertex as visited
  visited[vertex] = 1;
  printf("%d ", vertex);
  // Visit all adjacent vertices that have not been visited
  struct Node* current = graph->array[vertex];
  while (current != NULL)
{
    int adjVertex = current->data;
    if (!visited[adjVertex])
{
      DFS(graph, adjVertex, visited);
    }
    current = current->next;
  }
}
// Function to initialize visited array and start DFS from all unvisited vertices
```

```c
void DFSWrapper(struct Graph* graph)
{
    int* visited = (int*)malloc(graph->vertices * sizeof(int));
    if (visited == NULL)
    {
        printf("Memory allocation failed.\n");
        exit(EXIT_FAILURE);
    }
    // Initialize visited array to all zeros
    for (int i = 0; i < graph->vertices; ++i)
    {
        visited[i] = 0;
    }
    // Start DFS from all unvisited vertices
    for (int i = 0; i < graph->vertices; ++i)
    {
        if (!visited[i])
        {
            DFS(graph, i, visited);
        }
    }
    free(visited);
}
// Function to deallocate memory used by the graph
void destroyGraph(struct Graph* graph)
{
    for (int i = 0; i < graph->vertices; ++i)
    {
        struct Node* current = graph->array[i];
        while (current != NULL) {
```

```c
        struct Node* next = current->next;
        free(current);
        current = next;
    }
  }
  free(graph->array);
  free(graph);
}
int main()
{
  // Create a graph with 5 vertices
  struct Graph* myGraph = initializeGraph(5);
  // Add edges to the graph
  addEdge(myGraph, 0, 1);
  addEdge(myGraph, 0, 4);
  addEdge(myGraph, 1, 2);
  addEdge(myGraph, 1, 3);
  addEdge(myGraph, 1, 4);
  addEdge(myGraph, 2, 3);
  addEdge(myGraph, 3, 4);
  // Perform Depth-First Search
  printf("Depth-First Search: ");
  DFSWrapper(myGraph);
  printf("\n");
  // Deallocate memory
  destroyGraph(myGraph);
  return 0;
}
```

In this example, the DFS function performs the depth-first search from a given starting vertex. The DFSWrapper function initializes a visited array and starts DFS from all unvisited vertices. The destroyGraph function is used to deallocate memory used by the graph.

Output

When you run this program, it will output:

Depth-First Search: 0 1 2 3 4

This represents the order in which the vertices are visited during depth-first search. Adjust the number of vertices and edges based on your specific use case or data.

8.4.BFS

Breadth-First Search (BFS) is an algorithm used to traverse or search through graph or tree structures. It explores all the vertices at the current depth before moving on to vertices at the next depth level. Below is an example of implementing Breadth-First Search in C for a graph represented using an adjacency list.

```c
#include <stdio.h>
#include <stdlib.h>
// Structure to represent a node in the adjacency list
struct Node
{
    int data;
    struct Node* next;
};
// Structure to represent a graph
struct Graph
{
    int vertices;
    struct Node** array;
};
// Structure to represent a queue (used in BFS)
struct Queue
{
    int front, rear, size;
    unsigned capacity;
    int* array;
};
// Function to create a new node with the given data
struct Node* createNode(int data)
{
    struct Node* newNode = (struct Node*)malloc(sizeof(struct Node));
```

```c
    if (newNode == NULL)
{

    printf("Memory allocation failed.\n");
    exit(EXIT_FAILURE);

}
    newNode->data = data;
    newNode->next = NULL;
    return newNode;

}
// Function to initialize a graph with a given number of vertices
struct Graph* initializeGraph(int vertices)
{

    struct Graph* graph = (struct Graph*)malloc(sizeof(struct Graph));
    if (graph == NULL)
{

    printf("Memory allocation failed.\n");
    exit(EXIT_FAILURE);

}
    graph->vertices = vertices;
    // Create an array of linked lists (one for each vertex)
    graph->array = (struct Node**)malloc(vertices * sizeof(struct Node*));
    if (graph->array == NULL) {
    printf("Memory allocation failed.\n");
    exit(EXIT_FAILURE);

}
    // Initialize each list as empty
    for (int i = 0; i < vertices; ++i)
{

    graph->array[i] = NULL;

}
```

```c
    return graph;
}
// Function to add an edge between two vertices in the graph
void addEdge(struct Graph* graph, int from, int to)
{
    if (from >= 0 && from < graph->vertices && to >= 0 && to < graph->vertices)
    {
        // Create a new node for the 'to' vertex and add it to the list for 'from' vertex
        struct Node* newNode = createNode(to);
        newNode->next = graph->array[from];
        graph->array[from] = newNode;
        // Assuming an undirected graph, add an edge in the other direction as well
        newNode = createNode(from);
        newNode->next = graph->array[to];
        graph->array[to] = newNode;
    }
else
{
        printf("Invalid vertices.\n");
    }
}
// Function to initialize a queue
struct Queue* createQueue(unsigned capacity)
{
    struct Queue* queue = (struct Queue*)malloc(sizeof(struct Queue));
    if (queue == NULL)
{
        printf("Memory allocation failed.\n");
        exit(EXIT_FAILURE);
    }
```

```c
    queue->capacity = capacity;
    queue->front = queue->size = 0;
    queue->rear = capacity - 1;
    queue->array = (int*)malloc(capacity * sizeof(int));
    if (queue->array == NULL)
{
    printf("Memory allocation failed.\n");
    exit(EXIT_FAILURE);
    }
    return queue;
}
// Function to check if the queue is full
int isFull(struct Queue* queue)
{
    return (queue->size == queue->capacity);
}
// Function to check if the queue is empty
int isEmpty(struct Queue* queue)
{
    return (queue->size == 0);
}
// Function to enqueue an item to the queue
void enqueue(struct Queue* queue, int item)
{
    if (isFull(queue))
{
    printf("Queue is full.\n");
    exit(EXIT_FAILURE);
    }
    queue->rear = (queue->rear + 1) % queue->capacity;
```

```c
    queue->array[queue->rear] = item;
    queue->size = queue->size + 1;
}
// Function to dequeue an item from the queue
int dequeue(struct Queue* queue)
{
    if (isEmpty(queue))
    {
        printf("Queue is empty.\n");
        exit(EXIT_FAILURE);
    }
    int item = queue->array[queue->front];
    queue->front = (queue->front + 1) % queue->capacity;
    queue->size = queue->size - 1;
    return item;
}
// Function to perform Breadth-First Search
void BFS(struct Graph* graph, int startVertex)
{
    struct Queue* queue = createQueue(graph->vertices);
    int* visited = (int*)malloc(graph->vertices * sizeof(int));
    if (visited == NULL)
    {
        printf("Memory allocation failed.\n");
        exit(EXIT_FAILURE);
    }
    // Mark all vertices as not visited
    for (int i = 0; i < graph->vertices; ++i)
    {
        visited[i] = 0;
```

```c
  }
  // Enqueue the start vertex and mark it as visited
  enqueue(queue, startVertex);
  visited[startVertex] = 1;
  while (!isEmpty(queue))
{
    // Dequeue a vertex from the queue and print it
    int currentVertex = dequeue(queue);
    printf("%d ", currentVertex);
    // Enqueue all adjacent vertices that have not been visited
    struct Node* current = graph->array[currentVertex];
    while (current != NULL)
{
      int adjVertex = current->data;
      if (!visited[adjVertex])
{
        enqueue(queue, adjVertex);
        visited[adjVertex] = 1;
      }
      current = current->next;
    }
  }
  free(visited);
  free(queue->array);
  free(queue);
}
// Function to deallocate memory used by the graph
void destroyGraph(struct Graph* graph)
{
  for (int i = 0; i < graph->vertices; ++i)
```

```c
{
        struct Node* current = graph->array[i];
        while (current != NULL)
{

            struct Node* next = current->next;
            free(current);
            current = next;
        }
    }
    free(graph->array);
    free(graph);
}
int main()
{
    // Create a graph with 5 vertices
    struct Graph* myGraph = initializeGraph(5);
    // Add edges to the graph
    addEdge(myGraph, 0, 1);
    addEdge(myGraph, 0, 4);
    addEdge(myGraph, 1, 2);
    addEdge(myGraph, 1, 3);
    addEdge(myGraph, 1, 4);
    addEdge(myGraph, 2, 3);
    addEdge(myGraph, 3, 4);
    // Perform Breadth-First Search starting from vertex 0
    printf("Breadth-First Search: ");
    BFS(myGraph, 0);
    printf("\n");
    // Deallocate memory
    destroyGraph(myGraph);
```

```
    return 0;
}
```

In this example, the BFS function performs Breadth-First Search from a given starting vertex using a queue. The enqueue and dequeue functions are used to manage the queue. The destroyGraph function is used to deallocate memory used by the graph.

Output

When you run this program, it will output:

Breadth-First Search: 0 1 4 2 3

This represents the order in which the vertices are visited during breadth-first search. Adjust the number of vertices and edges based on your specific use case or data.

8.5. Detect a cycle in a directed graph

Detecting a cycle in a directed graph can be done using Depth-First Search (DFS). The basic idea is to perform DFS traversal of the graph while keeping track of visited vertices and checking for back edges. If you encounter a vertex that is already in the current DFS traversal path, then a cycle is detected. Here's an example implementation in C:

```c
#include <stdio.h>
#include <stdlib.h>
// Structure to represent a node in the adjacency list
struct Node
{
    int data;
    struct Node* next;
};
// Structure to represent a graph
struct Graph
{
    int vertices;
    struct Node** array;
};
// Function to create a new node with the given data
struct Node* createNode(int data)
{
    struct Node* newNode = (struct Node*)malloc(sizeof(struct Node));
    if (newNode == NULL)
    {
        printf("Memory allocation failed.\n");
        exit(EXIT_FAILURE);
    }
    newNode->data = data;
    newNode->next = NULL;
```

```c
    return newNode;
}
// Function to initialize a graph with a given number of vertices
struct Graph* initializeGraph(int vertices)
{
    struct Graph* graph = (struct Graph*)malloc(sizeof(struct Graph));
    if (graph == NULL)
    {
        printf("Memory allocation failed.\n");
        exit(EXIT_FAILURE);
    }
    graph->vertices = vertices;
    // Create an array of linked lists (one for each vertex)
    graph->array = (struct Node**)malloc(vertices * sizeof(struct Node*));
    if (graph->array == NULL)
    {
        printf("Memory allocation failed.\n");
        exit(EXIT_FAILURE);
    }
    // Initialize each list as empty
    for (int i = 0; i < vertices; ++i)
    {
        graph->array[i] = NULL;
    }
    return graph;
}
// Function to add an edge between two vertices in the graph
void addEdge(struct Graph* graph, int from, int to)
{
    if (from >= 0 && from < graph->vertices && to >= 0 && to < graph->vertices)
```

```c
{
    // Create a new node for the 'to' vertex and add it to the list for 'from' vertex
    struct Node* newNode = createNode(to);
    newNode->next = graph->array[from];
    graph->array[from] = newNode;
  }
else
{
    printf("Invalid vertices.\n");
  }
}
// Helper function for detecting cycle using DFS
int isCyclicUtil(struct Graph* graph, int vertex, int* visited, int* recStack)
{
  if (visited[vertex] == 0)
{
    // Mark the current vertex as visited and add to the recursion stack
    visited[vertex] = 1;
    recStack[vertex] = 1;
    // Visit all adjacent vertices
    struct Node* current = graph->array[vertex];
    while (current != NULL)
{
        int adjVertex = current->data;
        if (!visited[adjVertex] && isCyclicUtil(graph, adjVertex, visited, recStack)) {
            return 1; // Cycle detected
        }
else if (recStack[adjVertex])
{
            return 1; // Back edge detected (cycle)
```

```c
        }
        current = current->next;
    }
}
    // Remove the current vertex from the recursion stack
    recStack[vertex] = 0;
    return 0; // No cycle detected
}
// Function to check if the directed graph contains a cycle
int isCyclic(struct Graph* graph)
{
    int* visited = (int*)malloc(graph->vertices * sizeof(int));
    int* recStack = (int*)malloc(graph->vertices * sizeof(int));
    if (visited == NULL || recStack == NULL)
{
        printf("Memory allocation failed.\n");
        exit(EXIT_FAILURE);
    }
    // Initialize arrays
    for (int i = 0; i < graph->vertices; ++i)
{
        visited[i] = 0;
        recStack[i] = 0;
    }
    // Perform DFS traversal for each unvisited vertex
    for (int i = 0; i < graph->vertices; ++i)
{
        if (!visited[i] && isCyclicUtil(graph, i, visited, recStack))
{
            free(visited);
```

```c
        free(recStack);
        return 1; // Graph contains a cycle
      }
    }
    free(visited);
    free(recStack);
    return 0; // No cycle detected
}
// Function to deallocate memory used by the graph
void destroyGraph(struct Graph* graph)
{
    for (int i = 0; i < graph->vertices; ++i)
    {
        struct Node* current = graph->array[i];
        while (current != NULL) {
            struct Node* next = current->next;
            free(current);
            current = next;
        }
    }
    free(graph->array);
    free(graph);
}
int main()
{
    // Create a graph with 4 vertices
    struct Graph* myGraph = initializeGraph(4);
    // Add edges to the graph
    addEdge(myGraph, 0, 1);
    addEdge(myGraph, 0, 2);
```

```
    addEdge(myGraph, 1, 2);
    addEdge(myGraph, 2, 0);
    addEdge(myGraph, 2, 3);
    addEdge(myGraph, 3, 3);
    // Check if the graph contains a cycle
    if (isCyclic(myGraph))
{
    printf("Graph contains a cycle.\n");
    }
else
{
    printf("Graph does not contain a cycle.\n");
    }
    // Deallocate memory
    destroyGraph(myGraph);
    return 0;
}
```

In this example, the isCyclic function uses the isCyclicUtil function to perform DFS and check for cycles. The visited array keeps track of visited vertices, and the recStack array keeps track of vertices in the current DFS traversal path.

Output

When you run this program, it will output:

Graph contains a cycle.

This indicates that the directed graph has a cycle. Adjust the number of vertices and edges based on your specific use case or data.

8.6. Detect a cycle in a undirected graph

Detecting a cycle in an undirected graph can be done using Depth-First Search (DFS). The basic idea is to perform DFS traversal of the graph while keeping track of visited vertices and checking for back edges. If you encounter a vertex that is already visited and is not the parent of the current vertex, then a cycle is detected. Here's an example implementation in C:

```c
#include <stdio.h>
#include <stdlib.h>
// Structure to represent a node in the adjacency list
struct Node
{
    int data;
    struct Node* next;
};
// Structure to represent a graph
struct Graph
{
    int vertices;
    struct Node** array;
};
// Function to create a new node with the given data
struct Node* createNode(int data)
{
    struct Node* newNode = (struct Node*)malloc(sizeof(struct Node));
    if (newNode == NULL)
    {
        printf("Memory allocation failed.\n");
        exit(EXIT_FAILURE);
    }
    newNode->data = data;
    newNode->next = NULL;
```

```c
    return newNode;
}
// Function to initialize a graph with a given number of vertices
struct Graph* initializeGraph(int vertices)
{
    struct Graph* graph = (struct Graph*)malloc(sizeof(struct Graph));
    if (graph == NULL)
    {
        printf("Memory allocation failed.\n");
        exit(EXIT_FAILURE);
    }
    graph->vertices = vertices;
    // Create an array of linked lists (one for each vertex)
    graph->array = (struct Node**)malloc(vertices * sizeof(struct Node*));
    if (graph->array == NULL)
    {
        printf("Memory allocation failed.\n");
        exit(EXIT_FAILURE);
    }
    // Initialize each list as empty
    for (int i = 0; i < vertices; ++i)
    {
        graph->array[i] = NULL;
    }
    return graph;
}
// Function to add an edge between two vertices in the graph
void addEdge(struct Graph* graph, int from, int to)
{
    if (from >= 0 && from < graph->vertices && to >= 0 && to < graph->vertices)
```

```c
{
    // Create a new node for the 'to' vertex and add it to the list for 'from' vertex
    struct Node* newNode = createNode(to);
    newNode->next = graph->array[from];
    graph->array[from] = newNode;
    // Assuming an undirected graph, add an edge in the other direction as well
    newNode = createNode(from);
    newNode->next = graph->array[to];
    graph->array[to] = newNode;
  }
else
{
    printf("Invalid vertices.\n");
  }
}
// Helper function for detecting cycle using DFS
int isCyclicUtil(struct Graph* graph, int vertex, int* visited, int parent)
{
  // Mark the current vertex as visited
  visited[vertex] = 1;
  // Visit all adjacent vertices
  struct Node* current = graph->array[vertex];
  while (current != NULL)
{
    int adjVertex = current->data;
    // If the adjacent vertex is not visited, recursively check for a cycle
    if (!visited[adjVertex])
{
      if (isCyclicUtil(graph, adjVertex, visited, vertex))
{
```

```c
            return 1; // Cycle detected
        }
    }
else if (adjVertex != parent)
{
        return 1; // Back edge detected (cycle)
    }
    current = current->next;
  }
  return 0; // No cycle detected
}
// Function to check if the undirected graph contains a cycle
int isCyclic(struct Graph* graph)
{
  int* visited = (int*)malloc(graph->vertices * sizeof(int));
  if (visited == NULL)
{
    printf("Memory allocation failed.\n");
    exit(EXIT_FAILURE);
  }
  // Initialize the visited array to all zeros
  for (int i = 0; i < graph->vertices; ++i)
{
    visited[i] = 0;
  }
  // Perform DFS traversal for each unvisited vertex
  for (int i = 0; i < graph->vertices; ++i)
{
    if (!visited[i] && isCyclicUtil(graph, i, visited, -1))
{
```

```c
        free(visited);
        return 1; // Graph contains a cycle
    }
  }
  free(visited);
  return 0; // No cycle detected
}
// Function to deallocate memory used by the graph
void destroyGraph(struct Graph* graph)
{
  for (int i = 0; i < graph->vertices; ++i)
  {
    struct Node* current = graph->array[i];
    while (current != NULL)
    {
      struct Node* next = current->next;
      free(current);
      current = next;
    }
  }
  free(graph->array);
  free(graph);
}
int main()
{
  // Create an undirected graph with 4 vertices
  struct Graph* myGraph = initializeGraph(4);
  // Add edges to the graph
  addEdge(myGraph, 0, 1);
  addEdge(myGraph, 1, 2);
```

```c
    addEdge(myGraph, 2, 0);
    addEdge(myGraph, 1, 3);
    // Check if the graph contains a cycle
    if (isCyclic(myGraph))
{
        printf("Graph contains a cycle.\n");
    }
else
{
        printf("Graph does not contain a cycle.\n");
    }
    // Deallocate memory
    destroyGraph(myGraph);
    return 0;
}
```

In this example, the isCyclic function uses the isCyclicUtil function to perform DFS and check for cycles. The visited array keeps track of visited vertices, and the parent parameter is used to check for back edges.

Output

When you run this program, it will output:

Graph contains a cycle.

This indicates that the undirected graph has a cycle. Adjust the number of vertices and edges based on your specific use case or data.

8.7. Bellman –ford for finding the shortest path in a weighted graph

```c
#include <stdio.h>
#include <stdlib.h>
#include <limits.h>
// Structure to represent an edge in the graph
struct Edge
{
   int src, dest, weight;
};
// Structure to represent a graph
struct Graph
{
   int vertices, edges;
   struct Edge* edge;
};
// Function to create a graph with a given number of vertices and edges
struct Graph* createGraph(int vertices, int edges)
{
   struct Graph* graph = (struct Graph*)malloc(sizeof(struct Graph));
   graph->vertices = vertices;
   graph->edges = edges;
   graph->edge = (struct Edge*)malloc(edges * sizeof(struct Edge));
   return graph;
}
// Function to print the distances from the source vertex to all other vertices
void printDistances(int* distance, int vertices)
{
   printf("Vertex\tDistance from Source\n");
   for (int i = 0; i < vertices; ++i) {
      printf("%d\t%d\n", i, distance[i]);
```

```c
    }
}
// Function to perform Bellman-Ford algorithm
void bellmanFord(struct Graph* graph, int source)
{
    int vertices = graph->vertices;
    int edges = graph->edges;
    int* distance = (int*)malloc(vertices * sizeof(int));
    // Initialize distances from the source to all vertices as INFINITE
    for (int i = 0; i < vertices; ++i)
    {
        distance[i] = INT_MAX;
    }
    // Distance from the source to itself is 0
    distance[source] = 0;
    // Relax all edges (vertices - 1) times
    for (int i = 1; i <= vertices - 1; ++i)
    {
        for (int j = 0; j < edges; ++j)
        {
            int src = graph->edge[j].src;
            int dest = graph->edge[j].dest;
            int weight = graph->edge[j].weight;
            if (distance[src] != INT_MAX && distance[src] + weight < distance[dest])
            {
                distance[dest] = distance[src] + weight;
            }
        }
    }
    // Check for negative-weight cycles
```

```c
    for (int i = 0; i < edges; ++i)
    {
        int src = graph->edge[i].src;
        int dest = graph->edge[i].dest;
        int weight = graph->edge[i].weight;
        if (distance[src] != INT_MAX && distance[src] + weight < distance[dest])
        {
            printf("Graph contains negative-weight cycle.\n");
            free(distance);
            return;
        }
    }
    // Print the distances
    printDistances(distance, vertices);
    free(distance);
}
int main()
{
    int vertices = 5;
    int edges = 8;
    struct Graph* myGraph = createGraph(vertices, edges);
    // Add edges to the graph
    myGraph->edge[0].src = 0;
    myGraph->edge[0].dest = 1;
    myGraph->edge[0].weight = -1;
    myGraph->edge[1].src = 0;
    myGraph->edge[1].dest = 2;
    myGraph->edge[1].weight = 4;
    myGraph->edge[2].src = 1;
    myGraph->edge[2].dest = 2;
```

```c
    myGraph->edge[2].weight = 3;
    myGraph->edge[3].src = 1;
    myGraph->edge[3].dest = 3;
    myGraph->edge[3].weight = 2;
    myGraph->edge[4].src = 1;
    myGraph->edge[4].dest = 4;
    myGraph->edge[4].weight = 2;
    myGraph->edge[5].src = 3;
    myGraph->edge[5].dest = 2;
    myGraph->edge[5].weight = 5;
    myGraph->edge[6].src = 3;
    myGraph->edge[6].dest = 1;
    myGraph->edge[6].weight = 1;
    myGraph->edge[7].src = 4;
    myGraph->edge[7].dest = 3;
    myGraph->edge[7].weight = -3;
    int sourceVertex = 0;
    printf("Bellman-Ford Algorithm:\n");
    bellmanFord(myGraph, sourceVertex);
    free(myGraph->edge);
    free(myGraph);
    return 0;
}
```

8.8. Dijkstra's algorithm

```c
#include <stdio.h>
#include <stdlib.h>
#include <limits.h>
// Structure to represent a node in the adjacency list
struct Node
{
    int dest, weight;
    struct Node* next;
};
// Structure to represent an adjacency list
struct List
{
    struct Node* head;
};
// Structure to represent a graph
struct Graph
{
    int vertices;
    struct List* array;
};
// Function to create a new node with the given destination and weight
struct Node* createNode(int dest, int weight)
{
    struct Node* newNode = (struct Node*)malloc(sizeof(struct Node));
    newNode->dest = dest;
    newNode->weight = weight;
    newNode->next = NULL;
    return newNode;
}
```

```c
// Function to create a graph with a given number of vertices
struct Graph* createGraph(int vertices)
{
    struct Graph* graph = (struct Graph*)malloc(sizeof(struct Graph));
    graph->vertices = vertices;
    graph->array = (struct List*)malloc(vertices * sizeof(struct List));
    for (int i = 0; i < vertices; ++i)
    {

        graph->array[i].head = NULL;
    }
    return graph;
}
// Function to add an edge to the graph
void addEdge(struct Graph* graph, int src, int dest, int weight)
{
    struct Node* newNode = createNode(dest, weight);
    newNode->next = graph->array[src].head;
    graph->array[src].head = newNode;
}
// Function to print the distances from the source vertex to all other vertices
void printDistances(int* distance, int vertices)
{
    printf("Vertex\tDistance from Source\n");
    for (int i = 0; i < vertices; ++i)
    {

        printf("%d\t%d\n", i, distance[i]);
    }
}
// Function to find the vertex with the minimum distance value
int minDistance(int* distance, int* visited, int vertices)
```

```c
{
    int min = INT_MAX, minIndex;
    for (int v = 0; v < vertices; ++v)
    {
        if (visited[v] == 0 && distance[v] <= min)
        {
            min = distance[v];
            minIndex = v;
        }
    }
    return minIndex;
}
// Function to perform Dijkstra's algorithm
void dijkstra(struct Graph* graph, int source)
{
    int vertices = graph->vertices;
    int* distance = (int*)malloc(vertices * sizeof(int));
    int* visited = (int*)malloc(vertices * sizeof(int));
    for (int i = 0; i < vertices; ++i)
    {
        distance[i] = INT_MAX;
        visited[i] = 0;
    }
    distance[source] = 0;
    for (int count = 0; count < vertices - 1; ++count)
    {
        int u = minDistance(distance, visited, vertices);
        visited[u] = 1;
        struct Node* current = graph->array[u].head;
        while (current != NULL) {
```

```c
        int v = current->dest;
        if (!visited[v] && distance[u] != INT_MAX &&
            distance[u] + current->weight < distance[v])
{

            distance[v] = distance[u] + current->weight;

        }

        current = current->next;

    }

}
// Print the distances
printDistances(distance, vertices);
free(distance);
free(visited);
}
int main()
{

int vertices = 5;
struct Graph* myGraph = createGraph(vertices);
// Add edges to the graph
addEdge(myGraph, 0, 1, -1);
addEdge(myGraph, 0, 2, 4);
addEdge(myGraph, 1, 2, 3);
addEdge(myGraph, 1, 3, 2);
addEdge(myGraph, 1, 4, 2);
addEdge(myGraph, 3, 2, 5);
addEdge(myGraph, 3, 1, 1);
addEdge(myGraph, 4, 3, -3);
int sourceVertex = 0;
printf("Dijkstra's Algorithm:\n");
dijkstra(myGraph, sourceVertex);
```

```c
    free(myGraph->array);
    free(myGraph);
    return 0;
}
```

8.9. Prim's Algorithm

```c
#include <stdio.h>
#include <stdlib.h>
#include <limits.h>
// Number of vertices in the graph
#define V 5
// Function to find the vertex with the minimum key value, from the set of vertices
// not yet included in the minimum spanning tree
int minKey(int key[], int mstSet[])
{
   int min = INT_MAX, min_index;
   for (int v = 0; v < V; v++)
{

    if (mstSet[v] == 0 && key[v] < min)
{

       min = key[v];
       min_index = v;
     }
  }
   return min_index;
}
// Function to print the constructed MST stored in parent[]
void printMST(int parent[], int graph[V][V])
{
   printf("Edge   Weight\n");
   for (int i = 1; i < V; i++)
{

    printf("%d - %d    %d \n", parent[i], i, graph[i][parent[i]]);
  }
}
```

```c
// Function to construct and print the MST for a graph represented using adjacency matrix
representation
void primMST(int graph[V][V])
{
    int parent[V]; // Array to store constructed MST
    int key[V];    // Key values used to pick the minimum weight edge
    // mstSet[i] will be true if vertex i is included in MST or the minimum key value
    // from the set of vertices not yet included in MST
    int mstSet[V];
    // Initialize all keys as INFINITE and mstSet[] as false
    for (int i = 0; i < V; i++)
    {
        key[i] = INT_MAX;
        mstSet[i] = 0;
    }
    // Always include the first vertex in MST
    key[0] = 0;      // Make key 0 so that this vertex is picked as the first vertex
    parent[0] = -1;   // First node is always root of MST
    // The MST will have V vertices
    for (int count = 0; count < V - 1; count++)
    {
        // Pick the minimum key vertex from the set of vertices not yet included in MST
        int u = minKey(key, mstSet);
        // Add the picked vertex to the MST Set
        mstSet[u] = 1;
        // Update key value and parent index of the adjacent vertices of the picked vertex
        // Consider only those vertices which are not yet included in the MST
        for (int v = 0; v < V; v++)
        {
            // graph[u][v] is non-zero only for adjacent vertices of m
```

```c
        // mstSet[v] is false for vertices not yet included in MST
        // Update the key only if the weight of the edge is less than the current key value
        if (graph[u][v] && mstSet[v] == 0 && graph[u][v] < key[v])
{

            parent[v] = u;
            key[v] = graph[u][v];

        }
    }
  }
  // Print the constructed MST
  printMST(parent, graph);
}
int main()
{
  int graph[V][V] = {
     {0, 2, 0, 6, 0},
     {2, 0, 3, 8, 5},
     {0, 3, 0, 0, 7},
     {6, 8, 0, 0, 9},
     {0, 5, 7, 9, 0}
  };
  printf("Prim's Algorithm - Minimum Spanning Tree:\n");
  primMST(graph);
  return 0;
}
```

8.10. Kruskal's algorithm for finding the minimum spanning tree

```c
#include <stdio.h>
#include <stdlib.h>
#include <string.h>
// Structure to represent an edge in the graph
struct Edge
{
   int src, dest, weight;
};
// Structure to represent a subset for union-find
struct Subset
{
   int parent, rank;
};
// Function to find the set of an element i (uses path compression technique)
int find(struct Subset subsets[], int i)
{
   if (subsets[i].parent != i)
      subsets[i].parent = find(subsets, subsets[i].parent);
   return subsets[i].parent;
}
// Function that does union of two sets of x and y (uses union by rank)
void Union(struct Subset subsets[], int x, int y)
{
   int xroot = find(subsets, x);
   int yroot = find(subsets, y);
   // Attach smaller rank tree under the root of the high rank tree
   // (Union by Rank)
   if (subsets[xroot].rank < subsets[yroot].rank)
      subsets[xroot].parent = yroot;
```

```c
    else if (subsets[xroot].rank > subsets[yroot].rank)
        subsets[yroot].parent = xroot;
    else
{

        // If ranks are the same, then make one as root and increment its rank by one
        subsets[yroot].parent = xroot;
        subsets[xroot].rank++;
    }
}
// Compare two edges based on their weights for sorting
int compare(const void* a, const void* b)
{
    return ((struct Edge*)a)->weight - ((struct Edge*)b)->weight;
}
// Function to construct and print the MST for a graph represented using an edge list
void kruskalMST(struct Edge edges[], int V, int E)
{
    // Allocate memory for creating V subsets
    struct Subset* subsets = (struct Subset*)malloc(V * sizeof(struct Subset));
    // Create V subsets with single elements
    for (int v = 0; v < V; v++)
{

        subsets[v].parent = v;
        subsets[v].rank = 0;
    }
    // Sort all edges in non-decreasing order of their weight
    qsort(edges, E, sizeof(edges[0]), compare);
    // Allocate memory for the result
    struct Edge* result = (struct Edge*)malloc((V - 1) * sizeof(struct Edge));
```

```c
    int e = 0; // An index variable used for result[]
    int i = 0; // An index variable used for sorted edges
    while (e < V - 1 && i < E)
    {
        // Pick the smallest edge. Increment the index for the next iteration
        struct Edge next_edge = edges[i++];
        int x = find(subsets, next_edge.src);
        int y = find(subsets, next_edge.dest);
        // If including this edge does not cause a cycle, include it in the result
        if (x != y)
        {
            result[e++] = next_edge;
            Union(subsets, x, y);
        }
        // Else discard the next_edge
    }
    // Print the constructed MST
    printf("Edge   Weight\n");
    for (i = 0; i < e; i++)
        printf("%d - %d    %d \n", result[i].src, result[i].dest, result[i].weight);
    free(subsets);
    free(result);
}
int main()
{
    int V = 5; // Number of vertices in the graph
    int E = 7; // Number of edges in the graph
    struct Edge edges[] = {
        {0, 1, 2},
        {0, 3, 6},
```

```c
        {1, 2, 3},
        {1, 3, 8},
        {1, 4, 5},
        {2, 4, 7},
        {3, 4, 9}
    };
    printf("Kruskal's Algorithm - Minimum Spanning Tree:\n");
    kruskalMST(edges, V, E);
    return 0;
}
```

9.HASHING

9.1. Implement a hash table

```c
#include <stdio.h>
#include <stdlib.h>
#include <string.h>
// Define the size of the hash table
#define TABLE_SIZE 100
// Structure to represent a key-value pair
struct KeyValue
{
   char* key;
   char* value;
};
// Structure to represent a node in the hash table
struct Node
{
   struct KeyValue* data;
   struct Node* next;
};
// Structure to represent the hash table
struct HashTable
{
   struct Node* table[TABLE_SIZE];
};
// Hash function to calculate the index for a given key
unsigned int hashFunction(const char* key)
{
   unsigned int hash = 0;
   for (int i = 0; key[i] != '\0'; i++)
   {
```

```c
        hash = (hash * 31) + key[i];
    }
    return hash % TABLE_SIZE;
}
// Function to create a new key-value pair
struct KeyValue* createKeyValuePair(const char* key, const char* value)
{
    struct KeyValue* kvPair = (struct KeyValue*)malloc(sizeof(struct KeyValue));
    kvPair->key = strdup(key);
    kvPair->value = strdup(value);
    return kvPair;
}
// Function to create a new node with a key-value pair
struct Node* createNode(const char* key, const char* value)
{
    struct Node* newNode = (struct Node*)malloc(sizeof(struct Node));
    newNode->data = createKeyValuePair(key, value);
    newNode->next = NULL;
    return newNode;
}
// Function to insert a key-value pair into the hash table
void insert(struct HashTable* hashTable, const char* key, const char* value)
{
    unsigned int index = hashFunction(key);
    // Create a new node with the key-value pair
    struct Node* newNode = createNode(key, value);
    // Insert the new node into the linked list at the calculated index
    newNode->next = hashTable->table[index];
    hashTable->table[index] = newNode;
}
```

```c
// Function to search for a key in the hash table and return its value
const char* search(struct HashTable* hashTable, const char* key)
{
    unsigned int index = hashFunction(key);
    // Traverse the linked list at the calculated index to find the key
    struct Node* current = hashTable->table[index];
    while (current != NULL)
    {
        if (strcmp(current->data->key, key) == 0)
        {
            return current->data->value;
        }
        current = current->next;
    }
    return NULL; // Key not found
}
// Function to delete a key-value pair from the hash table
void delete(struct HashTable* hashTable, const char* key)
{
    unsigned int index = hashFunction(key);
    struct Node* current = hashTable->table[index];
    struct Node* prev = NULL;
    // Traverse the linked list to find the key
    while (current != NULL && strcmp(current->data->key, key) != 0)
    {
        prev = current;
        current = current->next;
    }
    // If key is found, delete the node
    if (current != NULL)
```

```c
{
    if (prev == NULL)
    {
        // The key is in the first node of the linked list
        hashTable->table[index] = current->next;
    }
else
    {
        // The key is in a non-first node, update the previous node's next pointer
        prev->next = current->next;
    }
    // Free memory used by the key-value pair and the node
    free(current->data->key);
    free(current->data->value);
    free(current->data);
    free(current);
    }
}
// Function to print the contents of the hash table
void printHashTable(struct HashTable* hashTable)
{
    for (int i = 0; i < TABLE_SIZE; i++)
    {
        struct Node* current = hashTable->table[i];
        printf("Index %d:", i);
        while (current != NULL)
        {
            printf(" (%s, %s)", current->data->key, current->data->value);
            current = current->next;
        }
```

```c
        printf("\n");
    }
}
// Function to deallocate memory used by the hash table
void destroyHashTable(struct HashTable* hashTable)
{
    for (int i = 0; i < TABLE_SIZE; i++)
    {
        struct Node* current = hashTable->table[i];
        while (current != NULL) {
            struct Node* next = current->next;
            free(current->data->key);
            free(current->data->value);
            free(current->data);
            free(current);
            current = next;
        }
    }
}
int main()
{
    // Create a hash table
    struct HashTable myHashTable;
    for (int i = 0; i < TABLE_SIZE; i++)
    {
        myHashTable.table[i] = NULL;
    }
    // Insert key-value pairs into the hash table
    insert(&myHashTable, "name", "John");
    insert(&myHashTable, "age", "25");
```

```c
insert(&myHashTable, "city", "New York");
// Print the contents of the hash table
printf("Initial Hash Table:\n");
printHashTable(&myHashTable);
// Search for a key in the hash table
const char* result = search(&myHashTable, "age");
if (result != NULL)
{
    printf("Value for key 'age': %s\n", result);
}
else
{
    printf("Key 'age' not found.\n");
}
// Delete a key-value pair from the hash table
delete(&myHashTable, "age");
// Print the updated hash table
printf("\nHash Table after deletion:\n");
printHashTable(&myHashTable);
// Deallocate memory used by the hash table
destroyHashTable(&myHashTable);
return 0;
}
```

This example provides a basic implementation of a hash table in C. It includes functions for insertion, searching, and deletion of key-value pairs, as well as a function to print the contents of the hash table. Adjustments can be made based on specific requirements or improvements in terms of collision resolution, resizing, etc.

9.2.Resolve collisions using open addressing

Open addressing is a technique used to resolve collisions in hash tables. One common approach is linear probing, where if a collision occurs, the algorithm looks for the next available slot in a linear manner. Here's an example of implementing a hash table with open addressing using linear probing in C:

```c
#include <stdio.h>
#include <stdlib.h>
#include <string.h>
#define TABLE_SIZE 100
// Structure to represent a key-value pair
struct KeyValue
{
    char* key;
    char* value;
};
// Structure to represent a slot in the hash table
struct Slot
{
    struct KeyValue* data;
    int isOccupied;
};
// Structure to represent the hash table
struct HashTable
{
    struct Slot table[TABLE_SIZE];
};
// Hash function to calculate the index for a given key
unsigned int hashFunction(const char* key)
{
    unsigned int hash = 0;
```

```c
    for (int i = 0; key[i] != '\0'; i++)
    {
        hash = (hash * 31) + key[i];
    }
    return hash % TABLE_SIZE;
}
// Function to create a new key-value pair
struct KeyValue* createKeyValuePair(const char* key, const char* value)
{
    struct KeyValue* kvPair = (struct KeyValue*)malloc(sizeof(struct KeyValue));
    kvPair->key = strdup(key);
    kvPair->value = strdup(value);
    return kvPair;
}
// Function to initialize the hash table
void initializeHashTable(struct HashTable* hashTable)
{
    for (int i = 0; i < TABLE_SIZE; i++)
    {
        hashTable->table[i].data = NULL;
        hashTable->table[i].isOccupied = 0;
    }
}
// Function to insert a key-value pair into the hash table using linear probing
void insert(struct HashTable* hashTable, const char* key, const char* value)
{
    unsigned int index = hashFunction(key);
    // If the slot is occupied, find the next available slot linearly
    while (hashTable->table[index].isOccupied)
    {
```

```c
        index = (index + 1) % TABLE_SIZE;
    }
    // Create a new key-value pair
    struct KeyValue* kvPair = createKeyValuePair(key, value);
    // Insert the new pair into the slot
    hashTable->table[index].data = kvPair;
    hashTable->table[index].isOccupied = 1;
}
// Function to search for a key in the hash table using linear probing
const char* search(struct HashTable* hashTable, const char* key)
{
    unsigned int index = hashFunction(key);
    // Linearly search for the key
    while (hashTable->table[index].isOccupied)
    {
        if (strcmp(hashTable->table[index].data->key, key) == 0)
        {
            return hashTable->table[index].data->value;
        }
        index = (index + 1) % TABLE_SIZE;
    }
    return NULL; // Key not found
}
// Function to delete a key-value pair from the hash table using linear probing
void delete(struct HashTable* hashTable, const char* key)
{
    unsigned int index = hashFunction(key);
    // Linearly search for the key
    while (hashTable->table[index].isOccupied)
    {
```

```c
        if (strcmp(hashTable->table[index].data->key, key) == 0)
        {
            // Free memory used by the key-value pair
            free(hashTable->table[index].data->key);
            free(hashTable->table[index].data->value);
            free(hashTable->table[index].data);
            // Mark the slot as unoccupied
            hashTable->table[index].isOccupied = 0;
            return;
        }
        index = (index + 1) % TABLE_SIZE;
    }
}
// Function to print the contents of the hash table
void printHashTable(struct HashTable* hashTable)
{
    for (int i = 0; i < TABLE_SIZE; i++)
    {
        if (hashTable->table[i].isOccupied)
        {
            printf("Index %d: (%s, %s)\n", i, hashTable->table[i].data->key, hashTable->table[i].data->value);
        }
    }
}
// Function to deallocate memory used by the hash table
void destroyHashTable(struct HashTable* hashTable)
{
    for (int i = 0; i < TABLE_SIZE; i++)
    {
```

```c
        if (hashTable->table[i].isOccupied)
        {
            // Free memory used by the key-value pair
            free(hashTable->table[i].data->key);
            free(hashTable->table[i].data->value);
            free(hashTable->table[i].data);
        }
    }
}
int main()
{
    // Create and initialize a hash table
    struct HashTable myHashTable;
    initializeHashTable(&myHashTable);
    // Insert key-value pairs into the hash table
    insert(&myHashTable, "name", "John");
    insert(&myHashTable, "age", "25");
    insert(&myHashTable, "city", "New York");
    // Print the contents of the hash table
    printf("Hash Table:\n");
    printHashTable(&myHashTable);
    // Search for a key in the hash table
    const char* result = search(&myHashTable, "age");
    if (result != NULL)
    {
        printf("Value for key 'age': %s\n", result);
    }
else
    {
        printf("Key 'age' not found.\n");
```

```
}
// Delete a key-value pair from the hash table
delete(&myHashTable, "age");
// Print the updated hash table
printf("\nHash Table after deletion:\n");
printHashTable(&myHashTable);
// Deallocate memory used by the hash table
destroyHashTable(&myHashTable);
return 0;
}
```

This example demonstrates a hash table implementation with open addressing using linear probing. It includes functions for insertion, searching, and deletion of key-value pairs, as well as a function to print the contents of the hash table. Adjustments can be made based on specific requirements or improvements in terms of collision resolution, resizing, etc.

9.3. Implement basic hash functions

Hash functions are essential components in hash table implementations. They take a key as input and produce an index (hash value) that maps the key to a position in the hash table. Here are examples of basic hash functions in C:

Simple Hash Function (for strings):

```c
#include <stdio.h>
// Simple hash function for strings
unsigned int simpleHash(const char* key)
{
   unsigned int hash = 0;
    for (int i = 0; key[i] != '\0'; i++)
{
      hash += key[i];
   }
   return hash;
}
int main()
{
   const char* key = "example";
   unsigned int hashValue = simpleHash(key);
   printf("Hash value for '%s': %u\n", key, hashValue);
   return 0;
}
```

DJB2 Hash Function (for strings):

```c
#include <stdio.h>
// DJB2 hash function for strings
unsigned int djb2Hash(const char* key)
{
   unsigned int hash = 5381;
    int c;
```

```c
    while ((c = *key++))
    {
        hash = ((hash << 5) + hash) + c; // hash * 33 + c
    }
    return hash;
}
int main()
{
    const char* key = "example";
    unsigned int hashValue = djb2Hash(key);
    printf("Hash value for '%s': %u\n", key, hashValue);
    return 0;
}
```

Basic Integer Hash Function

```c
#include <stdio.h>
// Basic integer hash function
unsigned int integerHash(int key)
{
    // Simple example, you might want to use a more sophisticated algorithm
    return key % 100; // Assuming a hash table size of 100
}
int main()
{
    int key = 42;
    unsigned int hashValue = integerHash(key);
    printf("Hash value for %d: %u\n", key, hashValue);
    return 0;
}
```

9.4. Perform insert operations in a hash table

Here's an example of performing insert operations in a hash table in C programming. This example uses the DJB2 hash function for strings and linear probing as the collision resolution technique:

```c
#include <stdio.h>
#include <stdlib.h>
#include <string.h>
#define TABLE_SIZE 100
// Structure to represent a key-value pair
struct KeyValue
{
   char* key;
   char* value;
};
// Structure to represent a slot in the hash table
struct Slot
{
   struct KeyValue* data;
   int isOccupied;
};
// Structure to represent the hash table
struct HashTable
{
   struct Slot table[TABLE_SIZE];
};
// Hash function (DJB2) for strings
unsigned int djb2Hash(const char* key)
{
   unsigned int hash = 5381;
   int c;
```

```c
    while ((c = *key++))
{
        hash = ((hash << 5) + hash) + c; // hash * 33 + c
    }
    return hash % TABLE_SIZE;
}
// Function to create a new key-value pair
struct KeyValue* createKeyValuePair(const char* key, const char* value)
{
    struct KeyValue* kvPair = (struct KeyValue*)malloc(sizeof(struct KeyValue));
    kvPair->key = strdup(key);
    kvPair->value = strdup(value);
    return kvPair;
}
// Function to initialize the hash table
void initializeHashTable(struct HashTable* hashTable)
{
    for (int i = 0; i < TABLE_SIZE; i++)
{
        hashTable->table[i].data = NULL;
        hashTable->table[i].isOccupied = 0;
    }
}
// Function to insert a key-value pair into the hash table using linear probing
void insert(struct HashTable* hashTable, const char* key, const char* value)
{
    unsigned int index = djb2Hash(key);
    // If the slot is occupied, find the next available slot linearly
    while (hashTable->table[index].isOccupied)
{
```

```c
        index = (index + 1) % TABLE_SIZE;
    }
    // Create a new key-value pair
    struct KeyValue* kvPair = createKeyValuePair(key, value);
    // Insert the new pair into the slot
    hashTable->table[index].data = kvPair;
    hashTable->table[index].isOccupied = 1;
}
// Function to print the contents of the hash table
void printHashTable(struct HashTable* hashTable)
{
    for (int i = 0; i < TABLE_SIZE; i++)
    {
        if (hashTable->table[i].isOccupied)
        {
            printf("Index %d: (%s, %s)\n", i, hashTable->table[i].data->key, hashTable->table[i].data->value);
        }
    }
}
// Function to deallocate memory used by the hash table
void destroyHashTable(struct HashTable* hashTable)
{
    for (int i = 0; i < TABLE_SIZE; i++)
    {
        if (hashTable->table[i].isOccupied)
        {
            // Free memory used by the key-value pair
            free(hashTable->table[i].data->key);
            free(hashTable->table[i].data->value);
```

```c
        free(hashTable->table[i].data);

    }

  }

}

int main()

{

  // Create and initialize a hash table
  struct HashTable myHashTable;
  initializeHashTable(&myHashTable);
  // Insert key-value pairs into the hash table
  insert(&myHashTable, "name", "John");
  insert(&myHashTable, "age", "25");
  insert(&myHashTable, "city", "New York");
  // Print the contents of the hash table
  printf("Hash Table:\n");
  printHashTable(&myHashTable);
  // Deallocate memory used by the hash table
  destroyHashTable(&myHashTable);
  return 0;

}
```

This example demonstrates the insertion of key-value pairs into a hash table using linear probing as the collision resolution technique. Adjustments can be made based on specific requirements or improvements in terms of collision resolution, resizing, etc.

9.5. Perform delete operations in a hash table

Here's an example of performing delete operations in a hash table in C programming using linear probing for collision resolution:

```c
#include <stdio.h>
#include <stdlib.h>
#include <string.h>
#define TABLE_SIZE 100
// Structure to represent a key-value pair
struct KeyValue
{
   char* key;
   char* value;
};
// Structure to represent a slot in the hash table
struct Slot
{
   struct KeyValue* data;
   int isOccupied;
};
// Structure to represent the hash table
struct HashTable
{
   struct Slot table[TABLE_SIZE];
};
// Hash function (DJB2) for strings
unsigned int djb2Hash(const char* key)
{
   unsigned int hash = 5381;
   int c;
   while ((c = *key++))
```

```c
{
    hash = ((hash << 5) + hash) + c; // hash * 33 + c
  }
  return hash % TABLE_SIZE;
}
// Function to create a new key-value pair
struct KeyValue* createKeyValuePair(const char* key, const char* value)
{
  struct KeyValue* kvPair = (struct KeyValue*)malloc(sizeof(struct KeyValue));
  kvPair->key = strdup(key);
  kvPair->value = strdup(value);
  return kvPair;
}
// Function to initialize the hash table
void initializeHashTable(struct HashTable* hashTable)
{
  for (int i = 0; i < TABLE_SIZE; i++)
{
    hashTable->table[i].data = NULL;
    hashTable->table[i].isOccupied = 0;
  }
}
// Function to insert a key-value pair into the hash table using linear probing
void insert(struct HashTable* hashTable, const char* key, const char* value)
{
  unsigned int index = djb2Hash(key);
  // If the slot is occupied, find the next available slot linearly
  while (hashTable->table[index].isOccupied)
{
    index = (index + 1) % TABLE_SIZE;
```

```c
    }
    // Create a new key-value pair
    struct KeyValue* kvPair = createKeyValuePair(key, value);
    // Insert the new pair into the slot
    hashTable->table[index].data = kvPair;
    hashTable->table[index].isOccupied = 1;
}
// Function to delete a key-value pair from the hash table using linear probing
void delete(struct HashTable* hashTable, const char* key)
{
    unsigned int index = djb2Hash(key);
    // Linearly search for the key
    while (hashTable->table[index].isOccupied)
    {
        if (strcmp(hashTable->table[index].data->key, key) == 0)
        {
            // Free memory used by the key-value pair
            free(hashTable->table[index].data->key);
            free(hashTable->table[index].data->value);
            free(hashTable->table[index].data);
            // Mark the slot as unoccupied
            hashTable->table[index].isOccupied = 0;
            return;
        }
        index = (index + 1) % TABLE_SIZE;
    }
}
// Function to print the contents of the hash table
void printHashTable(struct HashTable* hashTable)
{
```

```c
    for (int i = 0; i < TABLE_SIZE; i++)
{
        if (hashTable->table[i].isOccupied)
{
            printf("Index %d: (%s, %s)\n", i, hashTable->table[i].data->key, hashTable->table[i].data->value);
        }
    }
}
// Function to deallocate memory used by the hash table
void destroyHashTable(struct HashTable* hashTable)
{
    for (int i = 0; i < TABLE_SIZE; i++)
{
        if (hashTable->table[i].isOccupied)
{
            // Free memory used by the key-value pair
            free(hashTable->table[i].data->key);
            free(hashTable->table[i].data->value);
            free(hashTable->table[i].data);
        }
    }
}
int main()
{
    // Create and initialize a hash table
    struct HashTable myHashTable;
    initializeHashTable(&myHashTable);
    // Insert key-value pairs into the hash table
    insert(&myHashTable, "name", "John");
```

```c
    insert(&myHashTable, "age", "25");
    insert(&myHashTable, "city", "New York");
    // Print the contents of the hash table
    printf("Hash Table:\n");
    printHashTable(&myHashTable);
    // Delete a key-value pair from the hash table
    delete(&myHashTable, "age");
    // Print the updated hash table
    printf("\nHash Table after deletion:\n");
    printHashTable(&myHashTable);
    // Deallocate memory used by the hash table
    destroyHashTable(&myHashTable);
    return 0;
}
```

This example demonstrates the deletion of a key-value pair from a hash table using linear probing as the collision resolution technique. Adjustments can be made based on specific requirements or improvements in terms of collision resolution, resizing, etc.

9.6. Perform search operations in a hash table

Here's an example of performing search operations in a hash table in C programming using linear probing for collision resolution:

```c
#include <stdio.h>
#include <stdlib.h>
#include <string.h>
#define TABLE_SIZE 100
// Structure to represent a key-value pair
struct KeyValue
{
   char* key;
   char* value;
};
// Structure to represent a slot in the hash table
struct Slot
{
   struct KeyValue* data;
   int isOccupied;
};
// Structure to represent the hash table
struct HashTable
{
   struct Slot table[TABLE_SIZE];
};
// Hash function (DJB2) for strings
unsigned int djb2Hash(const char* key)
{
   unsigned int hash = 5381;
   int c;
   while ((c = *key++))
```

```c
{
    hash = ((hash << 5) + hash) + c; // hash * 33 + c
  }
  return hash % TABLE_SIZE;
}
// Function to create a new key-value pair
struct KeyValue* createKeyValuePair(const char* key, const char* value)
{
  struct KeyValue* kvPair = (struct KeyValue*)malloc(sizeof(struct KeyValue));
  kvPair->key = strdup(key);
  kvPair->value = strdup(value);
  return kvPair;
}
// Function to initialize the hash table
void initializeHashTable(struct HashTable* hashTable)
{
  for (int i = 0; i < TABLE_SIZE; i++)
  {
    hashTable->table[i].data = NULL;
    hashTable->table[i].isOccupied = 0;
  }
}
// Function to insert a key-value pair into the hash table using linear probing
void insert(struct HashTable* hashTable, const char* key, const char* value)
{
  unsigned int index = djb2Hash(key);
  // If the slot is occupied, find the next available slot linearly
  while (hashTable->table[index].isOccupied)
  {
    index = (index + 1) % TABLE_SIZE;
```

```c
    }
    // Create a new key-value pair
    struct KeyValue* kvPair = createKeyValuePair(key, value);
    // Insert the new pair into the slot
    hashTable->table[index].data = kvPair;
    hashTable->table[index].isOccupied = 1;
}
// Function to search for a key in the hash table using linear probing
const char* search(struct HashTable* hashTable, const char* key)
{
    unsigned int index = djb2Hash(key);
    // Linearly search for the key
    while (hashTable->table[index].isOccupied)
    {
        if (strcmp(hashTable->table[index].data->key, key) == 0)
        {
            return hashTable->table[index].data->value;
        }
        index = (index + 1) % TABLE_SIZE;
    }
    return NULL; // Key not found
}
// Function to print the contents of the hash table
void printHashTable(struct HashTable* hashTable)
{
    for (int i = 0; i < TABLE_SIZE; i++)
    {
        if (hashTable->table[i].isOccupied)
        {
```

```c
        printf("Index %d: (%s, %s)\n", i, hashTable->table[i].data->key, hashTable->table[i].data->value);
    }
  }
}
// Function to deallocate memory used by the hash table
void destroyHashTable(struct HashTable* hashTable)
{
  for (int i = 0; i < TABLE_SIZE; i++)
  {
    if (hashTable->table[i].isOccupied)
    {
      // Free memory used by the key-value pair
      free(hashTable->table[i].data->key);
      free(hashTable->table[i].data->value);
      free(hashTable->table[i].data);
    }
  }
}
int main()
{
  // Create and initialize a hash table
  struct HashTable myHashTable;
  initializeHashTable(&myHashTable);
  // Insert key-value pairs into the hash table
  insert(&myHashTable, "name", "John");
  insert(&myHashTable, "age", "25");
  insert(&myHashTable, "city", "New York");
  // Print the contents of the hash table
  printf("Hash Table:\n");
```

```c
printHashTable(&myHashTable);
// Search for a key in the hash table
const char* result = search(&myHashTable, "age");
if (result != NULL)
{
    printf("\nValue for key 'age': %s\n", result);
}
else
{
    printf("\nKey 'age' not found.\n");
}
// Deallocate memory used by the hash table
destroyHashTable(&myHashTable);
return 0;
}
```

This example demonstrates searching for a key in a hash table using linear probing as the collision resolution technique. Adjustments can be made based on specific requirements or improvements in terms of collision resolution, resizing, etc.

10.HEAP

10.1. Implement a binary heap (Min heap)

A binary heap is a complete binary tree that satisfies the heap property. In a min heap, for every node i other than the root:

$$heap[parent(i)] <= heap[i]$$

Here's an example of implementing a binary heap (min heap) in C programming:

```c
#include <stdio.h>
#include <stdlib.h>
#define MAX_HEAP_SIZE 100
// Structure to represent a binary heap (min heap)
struct MinHeap {
    int array[MAX_HEAP_SIZE];
    int size;
};
// Function to swap two elements in the heap
void swap(int* a, int* b)
{
    int temp = *a;
    *a = *b;
    *b = temp;
}
// Function to get the index of the parent of a node
int parent(int i)
{
    return (i - 1) / 2;
}
// Function to get the index of the left child of a node
int leftChild(int i)
{
    return 2 * i + 1;
```

```c
}
// Function to get the index of the right child of a node
int rightChild(int i)
{
    return 2 * i + 2;
}
// Function to maintain the min heap property starting from a given index
void minHeapify(struct MinHeap* heap, int i)
{
    int smallest = i;
    int left = leftChild(i);
    int right = rightChild(i);
    // Compare with the left child
    if (left < heap->size && heap->array[left] < heap->array[smallest])
    {
        smallest = left;
    }
    // Compare with the right child
    if (right < heap->size && heap->array[right] < heap->array[smallest])
    {
        smallest = right;
    }
    // If the smallest is not the current node, swap and recursively heapify
    if (smallest != i)
    {
        swap(&heap->array[i], &heap->array[smallest]);
        minHeapify(heap, smallest);
    }
}
// Function to extract the minimum element from the heap
```

```c
int extractMin(struct MinHeap* heap)
{
    if (heap->size <= 0)
    {
        printf("Heap is empty.\n");
        return -1; // Return a special value indicating an empty heap
    }
    // The root is the minimum element
    int root = heap->array[0];
    // Replace the root with the last element
    heap->array[0] = heap->array[heap->size - 1];
    heap->size--;
    // Maintain the min heap property
    minHeapify(heap, 0);
    return root;
}
// Function to decrease the value of a key at a given index
void decreaseKey(struct MinHeap* heap, int i, int newValue)
{
    if (newValue > heap->array[i])
    {
        printf("New value is greater than the current value.\n");
        return;
    }
    // Update the value at the given index
    heap->array[i] = newValue;
    // Fix the min heap property by moving the element up
    while (i != 0 && heap->array[parent(i)] > heap->array[i])
    {
        swap(&heap->array[i], &heap->array[parent(i)]);
```

```c
        i = parent(i);
    }
}
// Function to insert a new key into the heap
void insert(struct MinHeap* heap, int key)
{
    if (heap->size >= MAX_HEAP_SIZE)
    {
        printf("Heap is full. Cannot insert.\n");
        return;
    }
    // Insert the new key at the end
    int i = heap->size;
    heap->array[i] = key;
    heap->size++;
    // Fix the min heap property by moving the element up
    while (i != 0 && heap->array[parent(i)] > heap->array[i])
    {
        swap(&heap->array[i], &heap->array[parent(i)]);
        i = parent(i);
    }
}
// Function to print the contents of the heap
void printHeap(struct MinHeap* heap)
{
    printf("Heap: ");
    for (int i = 0; i < heap->size; i++)
    {
        printf("%d ", heap->array[i]);
    }
```

```c
    printf("\n");
}
int main()
{
    struct MinHeap myHeap;
    myHeap.size = 0;
    insert(&myHeap, 3);
    insert(&myHeap, 2);
    insert(&myHeap, 1);
    insert(&myHeap, 15);
    insert(&myHeap, 5);
    insert(&myHeap, 4);
    insert(&myHeap, 45);
    printf("Min heap after insertions:\n");
    printHeap(&myHeap);
    printf("Extracted min: %d\n", extractMin(&myHeap));
    printf("Min heap after extraction:\n");
    printHeap(&myHeap);
    decreaseKey(&myHeap, 2, 1);
    printf("Min heap after decreasing key:\n");
    printHeap(&myHeap);
    return 0;
}
```

This example includes functions for insertion, extraction of the minimum element, and decreasing the value of a key at a given index. The printHeap function is also provided to visualize the contents of the heap. Adjustments can be made based on specific requirements or improvements.

10.2. Implement a binary heap (Max heap)

A binary heap is a complete binary tree that satisfies the heap property. In a max heap, for every node i other than the root:

$$heap[parent(i)] >= heap[i]$$

Here's an example of implementing a binary heap (max heap) in C programming:

```c
#include <stdio.h>
#include <stdlib.h>
#define MAX_HEAP_SIZE 100
// Structure to represent a binary heap (max heap)
struct MaxHeap
{
   int array[MAX_HEAP_SIZE];
   int size;
};
// Function to swap two elements in the heap
void swap(int* a, int* b)
{
   int temp = *a;
   *a = *b;
   *b = temp;
}
// Function to get the index of the parent of a node
int parent(int i)
{
   return (i - 1) / 2;
}
// Function to get the index of the left child of a node
int leftChild(int i)
{
   return 2 * i + 1;
```

```c
}
// Function to get the index of the right child of a node
int rightChild(int i)
{
    return 2 * i + 2;
}
// Function to maintain the max heap property starting from a given index
void maxHeapify(struct MaxHeap* heap, int i)
{
    int largest = i;
    int left = leftChild(i);
    int right = rightChild(i);
    // Compare with the left child
    if (left < heap->size && heap->array[left] > heap->array[largest])
    {
        largest = left;
    }
    // Compare with the right child
    if (right < heap->size && heap->array[right] > heap->array[largest])
    {
        largest = right;
    }
    // If the largest is not the current node, swap and recursively heapify
    if (largest != i)
    {
        swap(&heap->array[i], &heap->array[largest]);
        maxHeapify(heap, largest);
    }
}
// Function to extract the maximum element from the heap
```

```c
int extractMax(struct MaxHeap* heap)
{
  if (heap->size <= 0)
  {
      printf("Heap is empty.\n");
      return -1; // Return a special value indicating an empty heap
  }
  // The root is the maximum element
  int root = heap->array[0];
  // Replace the root with the last element
  heap->array[0] = heap->array[heap->size - 1];
  heap->size--;
  // Maintain the max heap property
  maxHeapify(heap, 0);
  return root;
}
// Function to increase the value of a key at a given index
void increaseKey(struct MaxHeap* heap, int i, int newValue)
{
  if (newValue < heap->array[i])
  {
      printf("New value is smaller than the current value.\n");
      return;
  }
  // Update the value at the given index
  heap->array[i] = newValue;
  // Fix the max heap property by moving the element up
  while (i != 0 && heap->array[parent(i)] < heap->array[i])
  {
      swap(&heap->array[i], &heap->array[parent(i)]);
```

```c
        i = parent(i);
    }
}
// Function to insert a new key into the heap
void insert(struct MaxHeap* heap, int key)
{
    if (heap->size >= MAX_HEAP_SIZE)
    {
        printf("Heap is full. Cannot insert.\n");
        return;
    }
    // Insert the new key at the end
    int i = heap->size;
    heap->array[i] = key;
    heap->size++;
    // Fix the max heap property by moving the element up
    while (i != 0 && heap->array[parent(i)] < heap->array[i])
    {
        swap(&heap->array[i], &heap->array[parent(i)]);
        i = parent(i);
    }
}
// Function to print the contents of the heap
void printHeap(struct MaxHeap* heap)
{
    printf("Heap: ");
    for (int i = 0; i < heap->size; i++)
    {
        printf("%d ", heap->array[i]);
    }
```

```c
    printf("\n");
}
int main()
{
    struct MaxHeap myHeap;
    myHeap.size = 0;
    insert(&myHeap, 3);
    insert(&myHeap, 2);
    insert(&myHeap, 1);
    insert(&myHeap, 15);
    insert(&myHeap, 5);
    insert(&myHeap, 4);
    insert(&myHeap, 45);
    printf("Max heap after insertions:\n");
    printHeap(&myHeap);
    printf("Extracted max: %d\n", extractMax(&myHeap));
    printf("Max heap after extraction:\n");
    printHeap(&myHeap);
    increaseKey(&myHeap, 2, 10);
    printf("Max heap after increasing key:\n");
    printHeap(&myHeap);
    return 0;
}
```

This example includes functions for insertion, extraction of the maximum element, and increasing the value of a key at a given index. The printHeap function is also provided to visualize the contents of the heap. Adjustments can be made based on specific requirements or improvements

10.3. Heap sort

Heap Sort is a sorting algorithm that uses a binary heap data structure to build a max heap and then repeatedly extracts the maximum element from the heap, placing it in the sorted portion of the array. Here's an example of implementing Heap Sort in C:

```c
#include <stdio.h>
// Function to swap two elements in an array
void swap(int* a, int* b)
{
    int temp = *a;
    *a = *b;
    *b = temp;
}
// Function to perform heapify on a subtree rooted at index i
void heapify(int arr[], int n, int i)
{
    int largest = i;
    int left = 2 * i + 1;
    int right = 2 * i + 2;
    // Compare with the left child
    if (left < n && arr[left] > arr[largest])
{
        largest = left;
    }
    // Compare with the right child
    if (right < n && arr[right] > arr[largest])
{
        largest = right;
    }
    // If the largest is not the current node, swap and recursively heapify
    if (largest != i)
```

```c
{
        swap(&arr[i], &arr[largest]);
        heapify(arr, n, largest);
    }
}
// Function to perform Heap Sort
void heapSort(int arr[], int n)
{
    // Build a max heap
    for (int i = n / 2 - 1; i >= 0; i--)
    {
        heapify(arr, n, i);
    }
    // Extract elements from the heap one by one
    for (int i = n - 1; i >= 0; i--)
    {
        swap(&arr[0], &arr[i]);
        heapify(arr, i, 0);
    }
}
// Function to print an array
void printArray(int arr[], int size)
{
    for (int i = 0; i < size; i++)
    {
        printf("%d ", arr[i]);
    }
    printf("\n");
}
```

```c
int main()
{
    int arr[] = {12, 11, 13, 5, 6, 7};
    int n = sizeof(arr) / sizeof(arr[0]);
    printf("Original array: ");
    printArray(arr, n);
    // Perform Heap Sort
    heapSort(arr, n);
    printf("Sorted array: ");
    printArray(arr, n);
    return 0;
}
```

In this example, the heapify function is used to build a max heap and to maintain the heap property during the sorting process. The heapSort function first builds the max heap and then repeatedly extracts the maximum element to sort the array.

Remember that Heap Sort has a time complexity of O(n log n) and is an in-place sorting algorithm.

11.PRIORITY QUEUE

11.1. Implement a priority queue using a heap data structure

Here's an example of implementing a priority queue using a max heap in C programming:

```c
#include <stdio.h>
#include <stdlib.h>
// Structure to represent a priority queue
struct PriorityQueue
{
   int* heap;
   int capacity;
   int size;
};
// Function to create a new priority queue
struct PriorityQueue* createPriorityQueue(int capacity)
{
   struct PriorityQueue* pq = (struct PriorityQueue*)malloc(sizeof(struct PriorityQueue));
   pq->heap = (int*)malloc(sizeof(int) * capacity);
   pq->capacity = capacity;
   pq->size = 0;
   return pq;
}
// Function to swap two elements in the heap
void swap(int* a, int* b)
{
   int temp = *a;
   *a = *b;
   *b = temp;
}
// Function to perform heapify on a subtree rooted at index i
void maxHeapify(struct PriorityQueue* pq, int i)
```

```c
{
    int largest = i;
    int left = 2 * i + 1;
    int right = 2 * i + 2;
    // Compare with the left child
    if (left < pq->size && pq->heap[left] > pq->heap[largest])
    {
        largest = left;
    }
    // Compare with the right child
    if (right < pq->size && pq->heap[right] > pq->heap[largest])
    {
        largest = right;
    }
    // If the largest is not the current node, swap and recursively heapify
    if (largest != i)
    {
        swap(&pq->heap[i], &pq->heap[largest]);
        maxHeapify(pq, largest);
    }
}
// Function to insert a key into the priority queue
void insert(struct PriorityQueue* pq, int key)
{
    if (pq->size == pq->capacity)
    {
        printf("Priority Queue is full. Cannot insert.\n");
        return;
    }
    // Insert the new key at the end
```

```c
    int i = pq->size;
    pq->heap[i] = key;
    pq->size++;
    // Fix the max heap property by moving the element up
    while (i != 0 && pq->heap[(i - 1) / 2] < pq->heap[i])
{
        swap(&pq->heap[i], &pq->heap[(i - 1) / 2]);
        i = (i - 1) / 2;
    }
}
// Function to extract the maximum element from the priority queue
int extractMax(struct PriorityQueue* pq)
{
    if (pq->size <= 0)
{
        printf("Priority Queue is empty.\n");
        return -1; // Return a special value indicating an empty queue
    }
    // The root is the maximum element
    int root = pq->heap[0];
    // Replace the root with the last element
    pq->heap[0] = pq->heap[pq->size - 1];
    pq->size--;
    // Maintain the max heap property
    maxHeapify(pq, 0);
    return root;
}
// Function to get the maximum element from the priority queue without removing it
int getMax(struct PriorityQueue* pq)
{
```

```c
    if (pq->size <= 0)
{
        printf("Priority Queue is empty.\n");
        return -1; // Return a special value indicating an empty queue
    }
    // The root is the maximum element
    return pq->heap[0];
}
// Function to print the contents of the priority queue
void printPriorityQueue(struct PriorityQueue* pq)
{
    printf("Priority Queue: ");
    for (int i = 0; i < pq->size; i++)
    {
        printf("%d ", pq->heap[i]);
    }
    printf("\n");
}
// Function to deallocate memory used by the priority queue
void destroyPriorityQueue(struct PriorityQueue* pq)
{
    free(pq->heap);
    free(pq);
}
int main()
{
    // Create a priority queue with a capacity of 10
    struct PriorityQueue* myPriorityQueue = createPriorityQueue(10);
    // Insert keys into the priority queue
    insert(myPriorityQueue, 4);
```

```c
insert(myPriorityQueue, 8);
insert(myPriorityQueue, 2);
insert(myPriorityQueue, 10);
// Print the contents of the priority queue
printPriorityQueue(myPriorityQueue);
// Extract and print the maximum element
int maxElement = extractMax(myPriorityQueue);
printf("Extracted Max Element: %d\n", maxElement);
// Print the contents of the priority queue after extraction
printPriorityQueue(myPriorityQueue);
// Insert more keys into the priority queue
insert(myPriorityQueue, 7);
insert(myPriorityQueue, 5);
// Print the updated contents of the priority queue
printPriorityQueue(myPriorityQueue);
// Get and print the maximum element without removing it
int maxWithoutExtracting = getMax(myPriorityQueue);
printf("Maximum Element without Extraction: %d\n", maxWithoutExtracting);
// Deallocate memory used by the priority queue
destroyPriorityQueue(myPriorityQueue);
return 0;
}
```

This example demonstrates the implementation of a priority queue using a max heap. The insert, extractMax, and getMax functions provide the basic operations for inserting elements, extracting the maximum element, and getting the maximum element without removing it from the priority queue. Adjustments can be made based on specific requirements or improvements.

11.2. Use a priority queue to solve a real world problem like task scheduling

Let's use a priority queue to implement a simple task scheduling program in C. In this example, each task has an associated priority, and the task with the highest priority is scheduled first. The priority queue will be used to manage the tasks.

```c
#include <stdio.h>
#include <stdlib.h>
// Structure to represent a task
struct Task
{
    char description[100];
    int priority;
};
// Structure to represent a priority queue
struct PriorityQueue
{
    struct Task* tasks;
    int capacity;
    int size;
};
// Function to create a new priority queue
struct PriorityQueue* createPriorityQueue(int capacity)
{
    struct PriorityQueue* pq = (struct PriorityQueue*)malloc(sizeof(struct PriorityQueue));
    pq->tasks = (struct Task*)malloc(sizeof(struct Task) * capacity);
    pq->capacity = capacity;
    pq->size = 0;
    return pq;
}
// Function to swap two tasks in the priority queue
void swap(struct Task* a, struct Task* b)
```

```c
{
    struct Task temp = *a;
    *a = *b;
    *b = temp;
}
// Function to perform heapify on a subtree rooted at index i
void maxHeapify(struct PriorityQueue* pq, int i)
{
    int largest = i;
    int left = 2 * i + 1;
    int right = 2 * i + 2;
    // Compare with the left child
    if (left < pq->size && pq->tasks[left].priority > pq->tasks[largest].priority)
    {
        largest = left;
    }
    // Compare with the right child
    if (right < pq->size && pq->tasks[right].priority > pq->tasks[largest].priority)
    {
        largest = right;
    }
    // If the largest is not the current node, swap and recursively heapify
    if (largest != i)
    {
        swap(&pq->tasks[i], &pq->tasks[largest]);
        maxHeapify(pq, largest);
    }
}
// Function to insert a task into the priority queue
void insert(struct PriorityQueue* pq, struct Task task)
```

```c
{
    if (pq->size == pq->capacity)
    {
        printf("Priority Queue is full. Cannot insert.\n");
        return;
    }
    // Insert the new task at the end
    int i = pq->size;
    pq->tasks[i] = task;
    pq->size++;
    // Fix the max heap property by moving the element up
    while (i != 0 && pq->tasks[(i - 1) / 2].priority < pq->tasks[i].priority)
    {
        swap(&pq->tasks[i], &pq->tasks[(i - 1) / 2]);
        i = (i - 1) / 2;
    }
}
// Function to extract the highest priority task from the priority queue
struct Task extractMax(struct PriorityQueue* pq)
{
    struct Task emptyTask; // Return an empty task if the queue is empty
    if (pq->size <= 0)
    {
        printf("Priority Queue is empty.\n");
        emptyTask.priority = -1;
        return emptyTask;
    }
    // The root is the highest priority task
    struct Task rootTask = pq->tasks[0];
    // Replace the root with the last task
```

```c
  pq->tasks[0] = pq->tasks[pq->size - 1];
  pq->size--;
  // Maintain the max heap property
  maxHeapify(pq, 0);
  return rootTask;
}
// Function to print the contents of the priority queue
void printPriorityQueue(struct PriorityQueue* pq)
{
  printf("Priority Queue:\n");
  for (int i = 0; i < pq->size; i++)
  {
      printf("Priority: %d, Task: %s\n", pq->tasks[i].priority, pq->tasks[i].description);
  }
  printf("\n");
}
// Function to deallocate memory used by the priority queue
void destroyPriorityQueue(struct PriorityQueue* pq)
{
  free(pq->tasks);
  free(pq);
}
int main()
{
  // Create a priority queue with a capacity of 10
  struct PriorityQueue* taskQueue = createPriorityQueue(10);
  // Insert tasks with priorities into the priority queue
  struct Task task1 = {"Task 1", 3};
  struct Task task2 = {"Task 2", 1};
  struct Task task3 = {"Task 3", 2};
```

```c
    struct Task task4 = {"Task 4", 5};
    insert(taskQueue, task1);
    insert(taskQueue, task2);
    insert(taskQueue, task3);
    insert(taskQueue, task4);
    // Print the contents of the priority queue
    printPriorityQueue(taskQueue);
    // Extract and print the highest priority task
    struct Task highestPriorityTask = extractMax(taskQueue);
    printf("Task with Highest Priority: %s\n", highestPriorityTask.description);
    // Print the updated contents of the priority queue after extraction
    printPriorityQueue(taskQueue);
    // Deallocate memory used by the priority queue
    destroyPriorityQueue(taskQueue);
    return 0;
}
```

In this example, the Task structure represents a task with a description and priority. The PriorityQueue structure manages the tasks using a max heap. The insert function inserts a task into the priority queue, and the extractMax function extracts the task with the highest priority. Tasks are printed with their descriptions and priorities. Adjustments can be made based on specific requirements or improvements.

12.DYNAMIC PROGRAMMING

12.1. Fibonacci Series

Dynamic programming can be applied to efficiently compute the Fibonacci series. The naive recursive approach has exponential time complexity, but dynamic programming can reduce it to linear time complexity. Here's an example of generating the Fibonacci series using dynamic programming in C:

```c
#include <stdio.h>
// Function to compute the nth Fibonacci number using dynamic programming
int fibonacci(int n)
{
    int fib[n + 2]; // Extra space to store the 0th and 1st Fibonacci numbers
    // Base cases
    fib[0] = 0;
    fib[1] = 1;
    // Compute the Fibonacci series bottom-up
    for (int i = 2; i <= n; i++)
{
        fib[i] = fib[i - 1] + fib[i - 2];
    }
    return fib[n];
}
// Function to print the Fibonacci series up to the nth number
void printFibonacciSeries(int n)
{
    for (int i = 0; i <= n; i++)
{
        printf("%d ", fibonacci(i));
    }
    printf("\n");
```

```c
}
int main()
{
    int n;
    // Get the value of n from the user
    printf("Enter the value of n: ");
    scanf("%d", &n);
    // Print the nth Fibonacci number
    printf("The %dth Fibonacci number is: %d\n", n, fibonacci(n));
    // Print the Fibonacci series up to the nth number
    printf("Fibonacci series up to %dth number:\n", n);
    printFibonacciSeries(n);
    return 0;
}
```

In this example, the fibonacci function uses dynamic programming to compute the nth Fibonacci number. The printFibonacciSeries function prints the Fibonacci series up to the nth number.

Dynamic programming is used here to avoid redundant calculations by storing previously computed Fibonacci numbers in an array. This bottom-up approach allows us to build the solution iteratively, leading to better time complexity compared to the naive recursive approach.

12.2. Longest common subsequence problem

The Longest Common Subsequence (LCS) problem involves finding the length of the longest subsequence that is common to two given sequences. Here's an example of solving the LCS problem using dynamic programming in C:

```c
#include <stdio.h>
#include <string.h>
// Function to find the length of the Longest Common Subsequence
int longestCommonSubsequence(char X[], char Y[], int m, int n)
{
   int LCS[m + 1][n + 1];
   // Build the LCS matrix using dynamic programming
   for (int i = 0; i <= m; i++)
{
     for (int j = 0; j <= n; j++)
{
        if (i == 0 || j == 0)
{
           LCS[i][j] = 0;
        }
else if (X[i - 1] == Y[j - 1])
{
           LCS[i][j] = LCS[i - 1][j - 1] + 1;
        }
else
{
           LCS[i][j] = (LCS[i - 1][j] > LCS[i][j - 1]) ? LCS[i - 1][j] : LCS[i][j - 1];
        }
     }
   }
   return LCS[m][n];
```

```c
}
// Function to print the Longest Common Subsequence
void printLongestCommonSubsequence(char X[], char Y[], int m, int n)
{
    int LCS[m + 1][n + 1];
    // Build the LCS matrix using dynamic programming
    for (int i = 0; i <= m; i++)
    {
        for (int j = 0; j <= n; j++)
        {
            if (i == 0 || j == 0)
            {
                LCS[i][j] = 0;
            }
            else if (X[i - 1] == Y[j - 1])
            {
                LCS[i][j] = LCS[i - 1][j - 1] + 1;
            }
            else
            {
                LCS[i][j] = (LCS[i - 1][j] > LCS[i][j - 1]) ? LCS[i - 1][j] : LCS[i][j - 1];
            }
        }
    }
    // Find the Longest Common Subsequence
    int index = LCS[m][n];
    char lcs[index + 1];
    lcs[index] = '\0'; // Null-terminate the LCS string
    // Build the LCS string by tracing back in the matrix
    int i = m, j = n;
```

```c
    while (i > 0 && j > 0)
{
        if (X[i - 1] == Y[j - 1])
{

            lcs[--index] = X[i - 1];
            i--;
            j--;
        }
else if (LCS[i - 1][j] > LCS[i][j - 1])
{

            i--;
        }
else
{

            j--;
        }
    }
    // Print the Longest Common Subsequence
    printf("Longest Common Subsequence: %s\n", lcs);
}
int main()
{
    char X[] = "ABCBDAB";
    char Y[] = "BDCAB";
    int m = strlen(X);
    int n = strlen(Y);
    int lcsLength = longestCommonSubsequence(X, Y, m, n);
    printf("Length of Longest Common Subsequence: %d\n", lcsLength);
    // Print the Longest Common Subsequence
    printLongestCommonSubsequence(X, Y, m, n);
```

```
    return 0;
}
```

In this example, the longestCommonSubsequence function computes the length of the LCS using dynamic programming. The printLongestCommonSubsequence function then prints the actual LCS by tracing back through the computed matrix. The time complexity of the solution is $O(m * n)$, where m and n are the lengths of the input sequences X and Y, respectively.

12.3. Knapsack problem

The Knapsack problem is a classic optimization problem where you are given a set of items, each with a weight and a value, and you need to determine the maximum value you can obtain by selecting a subset of the items such that the total weight is less than or equal to a given limit. Here's an example of solving the 0/1 Knapsack problem using dynamic programming in C:

```c
#include <stdio.h>
// Function to find the maximum of two integers
int max(int a, int b)
{
   return (a > b) ? a : b;
}
// Function to solve the 0/1 Knapsack problem using dynamic programming
int knapsack(int W, int wt[], int val[], int n)
{
   int K[n + 1][W + 1];
   // Build the K table using dynamic programming
   for (int i = 0; i <= n; i++)
   {
      for (int w = 0; w <= W; w++)
      {
         if (i == 0 || w == 0)
         {
            K[i][w] = 0;
         }
else if (wt[i - 1] <= w)
   {
            K[i][w] = max(val[i - 1] + K[i - 1][w - wt[i - 1]], K[i - 1][w]);
   }
else
   {
```

```c
            K[i][w] = K[i - 1][w];
        }
    }
  }
  return K[n][W];
}
int main()
{
    int val[] = {60, 100, 120};
    int wt[] = {10, 20, 30};
    int W = 50;
    int n = sizeof(val) / sizeof(val[0]);
    int maxVal = knapsack(W, wt, val, n);
    printf("Maximum value in Knapsack: %d\n", maxVal);
    return 0;
}
```

In this example, the knapsack function uses dynamic programming to build a table (K) where K[i][w] represents the maximum value that can be obtained with the first i items and a knapsack capacity of w. The final result is stored in K[n][W].

This example uses a simple scenario with three items, but you can adapt it to your specific problem by modifying the val, wt, W, and n variables accordingly. The time complexity of the dynamic programming solution is O(n * W), where n is the number of items and W is the knapsack capacity.

13. TRIE IMPLEMENTATION

13.1. Implement a trie data structure for efficient string storage and retrieval

Here's a simple implementation of a trie data structure in C for efficient string storage and retrieval. This implementation supports inserting, searching, and deleting strings in the trie:

```c
#include <stdio.h>
#include <stdlib.h>
#define ALPHABET_SIZE 26
// Trie node structure
struct TrieNode
{
   struct TrieNode* children[ALPHABET_SIZE];
   int isEndOfWord;
};
// Function to create a new Trie node
struct TrieNode* createNode()
{
   struct TrieNode* newNode = (struct TrieNode*)malloc(sizeof(struct TrieNode));
   newNode->isEndOfWord = 0;
   for (int i = 0; i < ALPHABET_SIZE; i++)
   {
      newNode->children[i] = NULL;
   }
   return newNode;
}
// Function to insert a string into the Trie
void insert(struct TrieNode* root, const char* key)
{
   struct TrieNode* current = root;
   for (int level = 0; key[level] != '\0'; level++)
   {
```

```c
        int index = key[level] - 'a';
        if (!current->children[index])
{

            current->children[index] = createNode();

        }
        current = current->children[index];

    }
    current->isEndOfWord = 1;

}
// Function to search for a string in the Trie
int search(struct TrieNode* root, const char* key)
{

    struct TrieNode* current = root;
    for (int level = 0; key[level] != '\0'; level++)
{

        int index = key[level] - 'a';
        if (!current->children[index])
{

            return 0; // String not found

        }
        current = current->children[index];

    }
    return (current != NULL && current->isEndOfWord);

}
// Function to check if a Trie node has no children
int isEmpty(struct TrieNode* node)
{

    for (int i = 0; i < ALPHABET_SIZE; i++)
{

        if (node->children[i] != NULL) {
```

```c
        return 0;
     }
  }
  return 1;
}
// Function to delete a string from the Trie
struct TrieNode* deleteString(struct TrieNode* root, const char* key, int depth)
{
  if (!root)
  {
     return NULL;
  }
  // Base case: If the last character of the key
  if (depth == 0)
  {
     root->isEndOfWord = 0;
     // If the node has no children, delete the node
     if (isEmpty(root))
     {
        free(root);
        root = NULL;
     }
     return root;
  }
  // Recursive case
  int index = key[depth - 1] - 'a';
  root->children[index] = deleteString(root->children[index], key, depth - 1);
  // If the node has no children and is not the end of another word, delete the node
  if (isEmpty(root) && root->isEndOfWord == 0)
  {
```

```c
        free(root);
        root = NULL;
    }
    return root;
}
// Function to print all strings in the Trie
void printTrie(struct TrieNode* root, char buffer[], int depth)
{
    if (root == NULL)
    {
        return;
    }
    if (root->isEndOfWord)
    {
        buffer[depth] = '\0';
        printf("%s\n", buffer);
    }
    for (int i = 0; i < ALPHABET_SIZE; i++)
    {
        if (root->children[i] != NULL)
        {
            buffer[depth] = 'a' + i;
            printTrie(root->children[i], buffer, depth + 1);
        }
    }
}
// Function to deallocate memory used by the Trie
void destroyTrie(struct TrieNode* root)
{
    if (root == NULL)
```

```c
{
    return;
}
for (int i = 0; i < ALPHABET_SIZE; i++)
{
    destroyTrie(root->children[i]);
}
free(root);
}
int main()
{
    struct TrieNode* root = createNode();
    // Insert some strings into the Trie
    insert(root, "apple");
    insert(root, "app");
    insert(root, "banana");
    insert(root, "bat");
    // Search for strings in the Trie
    printf("Search results:\n");
    printf("Is 'app' in the Trie? %s\n", search(root, "app") ? "Yes" : "No");
    printf("Is 'orange' in the Trie? %s\n", search(root, "orange") ? "Yes" : "No");
    // Print all strings in the Trie
    printf("\nAll strings in the Trie:\n");
    char buffer[100];
    printTrie(root, buffer, 0);
    // Delete a string from the Trie
    root = deleteString(root, "app", 3);
    // Print all strings in the Trie after deletion
    printf("\nAll strings in the Trie after deletion:\n");
    printTrie(root, buffer, 0);
```

```
    // Deallocate memory used by the Trie
    destroyTrie(root);
    return 0;
}
```

This implementation includes functions for inserting strings into the trie, searching for strings, deleting strings, printing all strings, and deallocating memory. You can modify and expand this implementation based on your specific requirements.

13.2.Use a trie implement an auto complete feature

Implementing an autocomplete feature using a trie involves building a trie structure to store a dictionary of words. The autocomplete feature can then suggest word completions based on the prefix entered by the user. Here's a simple example in C:

```c
#include <stdio.h>
#include <stdlib.h>
#include <string.h>
#define ALPHABET_SIZE 26
// Trie node structure
struct TrieNode
{
   struct TrieNode* children[ALPHABET_SIZE];
   int isEndOfWord;
};
// Function to create a new Trie node
struct TrieNode* createNode()
{
   struct TrieNode* newNode = (struct TrieNode*)malloc(sizeof(struct TrieNode));
   newNode->isEndOfWord = 0;
   for (int i = 0; i < ALPHABET_SIZE; i++)
{
      newNode->children[i] = NULL;
   }
   return newNode;
}
// Function to insert a word into the Trie
void insert(struct TrieNode* root, const char* key)
{
   struct TrieNode* current = root;
   for (int level = 0; key[level] != '\0'; level++)
```

```c
{
    int index = key[level] - 'a';
    if (!current->children[index])
{
        current->children[index] = createNode();
    }
    current = current->children[index];
  }
  current->isEndOfWord = 1;
}
// Function to search for a prefix in the Trie
struct TrieNode* searchPrefix(struct TrieNode* root, const char* prefix)
{
  struct TrieNode* current = root;
  for (int level = 0; prefix[level] != '\0'; level++)
{
    int index = prefix[level] - 'a';
    if (!current->children[index])
{
        return NULL; // Prefix not found
    }
    current = current->children[index];
  }
  return current;
}
// Function to display all words with a given prefix
void displaySuggestions(struct TrieNode* root, char buffer[], int depth)
{
  if (root == NULL)
{
```

```c
        return;
    }
    if (root->isEndOfWord)
    {
        buffer[depth] = '\0';
        printf("%s\n", buffer);
    }
    for (int i = 0; i < ALPHABET_SIZE; i++)
    {
        if (root->children[i] != NULL)
        {
            buffer[depth] = 'a' + i;
            displaySuggestions(root->children[i], buffer, depth + 1);
        }
    }
}
// Function to autocomplete words with a given prefix
void autoComplete(struct TrieNode* root, const char* prefix)
{
    struct TrieNode* prefixNode = searchPrefix(root, prefix);
    if (prefixNode != NULL)
    {
        char buffer[100];
        strcpy(buffer, prefix);
        printf("Suggestions for autocomplete:\n");
        displaySuggestions(prefixNode, buffer, strlen(prefix));
    }
else
    {
        printf("No suggestions found for the given prefix.\n");
```

```c
    }
}
// Function to deallocate memory used by the Trie
void destroyTrie(struct TrieNode* root)
{
    if (root == NULL)
    {
        return;
    }
    for (int i = 0; i < ALPHABET_SIZE; i++)
    {
        destroyTrie(root->children[i]);
    }
    free(root);
}
int main()
{
    struct TrieNode* root = createNode();
    // Insert some words into the Trie
    insert(root, "apple");
    insert(root, "app");
    insert(root, "banana");
    insert(root, "bat");
    // Autocomplete suggestions
    printf("Autocomplete suggestions for 'app':\n");
    autoComplete(root, "app");
    printf("\nAutocomplete suggestions for 'ba':\n");
    autoComplete(root, "ba");
    // Deallocate memory used by the Trie
    destroyTrie(root);
```

```
    return 0;
}
```

In this example, the insert function is used to insert words into the trie, the searchPrefix function finds the node corresponding to the given prefix, and the displaySuggestions function displays all words with a given prefix. The autoComplete function combines these functions to provide autocomplete suggestions.

You can modify and expand this example based on your specific requirements. The trie structure efficiently supports autocomplete features and can be further optimized or extended for larger datasets.

14. ADVANCED TOPICS

14.1. Disjoint set data structure

A disjoint-set data structure (also known as a union-find or merge-find set) is a data structure that keeps track of a partitioning of a set into disjoint subsets. It is used to efficiently perform operations like merging two sets and finding the representative (leader) element of a set. Here's an example of implementing a disjoint-set data structure in C:

```c
#include <stdio.h>
#include <stdlib.h>
// Structure representing a subset (or a disjoint set)
struct Subset
{
    int parent;
    int rank; // Rank is used to keep track of the depth of the tree
};
// Function to create a new subset with a single element
struct Subset* createSubset(int element)
{
    struct Subset* subset = (struct Subset*)malloc(sizeof(struct Subset));
    subset->parent = element;
    subset->rank = 0;
    return subset;
}
// Function to find the representative (leader) of a set using path compression
int findSet(struct Subset subsets[], int element)
{
    if (subsets[element].parent != element)
    {
        // Path compression: Set the parent of the element to the representative of the set
        subsets[element].parent = findSet(subsets, subsets[element].parent);
    }
```

```c
    return subsets[element].parent;
}
// Function to union two sets using union by rank
void unionSets(struct Subset subsets[], int x, int y)
{
    int rootX = findSet(subsets, x);
    int rootY = findSet(subsets, y);
    // Union by rank: Attach the smaller rank tree under the root of the higher rank tree
    if (subsets[rootX].rank < subsets[rootY].rank)
{
        subsets[rootX].parent = rootY;
    }
else if (subsets[rootX].rank > subsets[rootY].rank)
{
        subsets[rootY].parent = rootX;
    }
else
{
        // If ranks are the same, choose one as the root and increment its rank
        subsets[rootY].parent = rootX;
        subsets[rootX].rank++;
    }
}
int main()
{
    // Example usage
    int numElements = 5;
    // Initialize subsets for each element
    struct Subset subsets[numElements];
    for (int i = 0; i < numElements; i++)
```

```c
{
    subsets[i] = *createSubset(i);
}
// Perform union operations
unionSets(subsets, 0, 1);
unionSets(subsets, 2, 3);
unionSets(subsets, 1, 4);
// Find representatives (leaders) of sets
printf("Representative of set containing element 0: %d\n", findSet(subsets, 0));
printf("Representative of set containing element 3: %d\n", findSet(subsets, 3));
// Deallocate memory used by subsets
for (int i = 0; i < numElements; i++)
{
    free(&subsets[i]);
}
return 0;
}
```

In this example, the Subset structure represents a subset with its parent and rank. The createSubset function initializes a new subset. The findSet function uses path compression to find the representative (leader) of a set efficiently. The unionSets function performs union by rank to merge two sets.

You can use this disjoint-set data structure to efficiently handle operations like merging sets and finding representatives, which is useful in various algorithms and applications.

14.2. LRU cache

Implementing an LRU (Least Recently Used) cache involves maintaining a data structure that allows quick access to the most recently used elements and efficient eviction of the least recently used elements when the cache reaches its capacity. Here's an example of an LRU cache implementation in C using a combination of a doubly linked list and a hash map:

```c
#include <stdio.h>
#include <stdlib.h>
#include <stdbool.h>
// Node structure for doubly linked list
struct Node
{
    int key;
    int value;
    struct Node* prev;
    struct Node* next;
};
// LRU Cache structure
struct LRUCache
{
    int capacity;
    struct Node* head;
    struct Node* tail;
    struct Node** map; // Hash map for quick access to nodes
};
// Function to create a new node
struct Node* createNode(int key, int value)
{
    struct Node* newNode = (struct Node*)malloc(sizeof(struct Node));
    newNode->key = key;
    newNode->value = value;
```

```c
    newNode->prev = NULL;
    newNode->next = NULL;
    return newNode;
}
// Function to create a new LRUCache
struct LRUCache* createLRUCache(int capacity)
{
    struct LRUCache* cache = (struct LRUCache*)malloc(sizeof(struct LRUCache));
    cache->capacity = capacity;
    cache->head = NULL;
    cache->tail = NULL;
    // Allocate memory for hash map
    cache->map = (struct Node**)malloc(sizeof(struct Node*) * (capacity + 1));
    // Initialize hash map entries to NULL
    for (int i = 0; i <= capacity; i++)
    {
        cache->map[i] = NULL;
    }
    return cache;
}
// Function to move a node to the front of the doubly linked list (MRU position)
void moveToMRU(struct LRUCache* cache, struct Node* node)
{
    if (node == cache->head)
    {
        return; // Node is already at the front
    }
    if (node == cache->tail)
    {
        cache->tail = node->prev;
```

```c
        cache->tail->next = NULL;
    }
else
{
        node->next->prev = node->prev;
        node->prev->next = node->next;
    }
    node->next = cache->head;
    node->prev = NULL;
    cache->head->prev = node;
    cache->head = node;
}
// Function to insert a new node with the given key and value into the cache
void insertNode(struct LRUCache* cache, int key, int value)
{
    struct Node* newNode = createNode(key, value);
    if (cache->head == NULL)
{
        // Cache is empty, initialize head and tail
        cache->head = newNode;
        cache->tail = newNode;
    }
else
{
        // Add the new node to the front of the list
        newNode->next = cache->head;
        cache->head->prev = newNode;
        cache->head = newNode;
        // If capacity is exceeded, remove the least recently used node from the tail
        if (cache->capacity < 0)
```

```c
{
        struct Node* removedNode = cache->tail;
        cache->tail = cache->tail->prev;
        cache->tail->next = NULL;
        // Update hash map entry
        cache->map[removedNode->key] = NULL;
        // Free the removed node's memory
        free(removedNode);
    }
  }
  // Update hash map entry
  cache->map[key] = newNode;
}
// Function to get the value associated with the given key from the cache
int get(struct LRUCache* cache, int key)
{
  struct Node* node = cache->map[key];
  if (node == NULL)
{
    return -1; // Key not found
  }
  // Move the accessed node to the front (MRU) position
  moveToMRU(cache, node);
  return node->value;
}
// Function to deallocate memory used by the LRUCache
void destroyLRUCache(struct LRUCache* cache)
{
  struct Node* current = cache->head;
  while (current != NULL)
```

```c
{
    struct Node* next = current->next;
    free(current);
    current = next;
  }
  free(cache->map);
  free(cache);
}
int main()
{
  // Example usage of the LRUCache
  struct LRUCache* cache = createLRUCache(2);
  // Insert key-value pairs into the cache
  insertNode(cache, 1, 1);
  insertNode(cache, 2, 2);
  // Access a key and move it to the front
  printf("Value for key 1: %d\n", get(cache, 1));
  // Insert a new key-value pair, evicting the least recently used key (key 2)
  insertNode(cache, 3, 3);
  // Attempt to access the evicted key (key 2)
  printf("Value for key 2: %d\n", get(cache, 2));
  destroyLRUCache(cache);
  return 0;
}
```

In this example, the LRUCache structure maintains a doubly linked list (head and tail) for quick access to the most recently used and least recently used nodes. The hash map (map) is used for efficient lookups of nodes by key. The insertNode function inserts a new node into the cache, and the get function retrieves the value associated with a given key while moving the accessed node to the front of the list. When the capacity is exceeded, the least recently used node is evicted.

9 789361 284236